A Passionate Life

A Passionate Life

W. H. H. Murray, From Preacher to Progressive

RANDALL S. BEACH

**EXCELSIOR
EDITIONS**

Cover: 1870 oil on canvas painting by Winslow Homer entitled *The Trapper* (from Wikimedia Commons).

Published by State University of New York Press, Albany

Excelsior Editions is an imprint of State University of New York Press

For information, contact State University of New York Press, Albany, NY
www.sunypress.edu

Library of Congress Cataloging-in-Publication Data

Name: Beach, Randall S., author.
Title: A passionate life : W.H.H. Murray, from preacher to progressive / Randall S. Beach.
Description: Albany : State University of New York Press, 2022. | Series: Excelsior editions | Includes bibliographical references and index.
Identifiers: LCCN 2022005554 | ISBN 9781438489353 (hardcover : alk. paper) | ISBN 9781438489346 (pbk. : alk. paper) | ISBN 9781438489360 (ebook)
Subjects: LCSH: Murray, W. H. H. (William Henry Harrison), 1840–1904. | Outdoor life—United States—History—19th century. | Outdoorsmen—United States—Biography. | Clergy—Massachusetts—Boston—Biography.
Classification: LCC GV191.52.M87 B43 2022 | DDC 200.92 [B]—dc23/eng/20220408
LC record available at https://lccn.loc.gov/2022005554

10 9 8 7 6 5 4 3 2 1

Contents

Acknowledgments

I would like to thank the library staff at the Adirondack Experience at the Museum on Blue Mountain Lake for their gracious help in accessing the museum's Murray archives. Also, thanks go out to Julie Laing who helped with editing earlier versions of this work.

Thanks to the great people at SUNY Press and a special thank you to my wife Sarah, whose support was critical to this work.

Introduction

William Henry Harrison Murray or "Adirondack Murray" as much of the late-nineteenth-century public, both admirers and detractors, called the man, was a Boston preacher who, in 1869, started a movement with the publication of his book *Adventures in the Wilderness, or Camp Life in the Adirondacks*. Murray's *Adventure in the Wilderness*, at once travel guide and storybook, advocated time in nature, specifically New York State's Adirondack Mountains, as an essential gateway to both physical and spiritual health. It is for this book and his advocacy of the importance of nature and camping to the health of modern industrial city-dwelling men and women that Murray was most well known during his lifetime, and, indeed, remembered today.

An examination of Murray's life reveals an individual of far more depth and interest, however. From the 1860s until his early-twentieth-century death, Murray was a famous preacher, popular writer and lecturer, an equine enthusiast, patent owner, publisher, businessman, lumberman, temperance advocate, free lover, women's right advocate, and advocate for educational reform. As one contemporary remarked, William Henry Harrison Murray was a miscellaneous man.

Murray's nineteenth-century exploits are at times tragic, comic and even bewildering. Indeed, his life can sometimes seem less probable than that of any of the characters he invented in his many books and stories. As a youth, Murray displayed characteristics of the young rascal, a trait he never fully grew outgrew. But while he surely displayed a talent for mischief, his ability to focus intensely on an object he was passionate about was also evident first in youth, and then throughout his life.

Murray was a man of passion. As a youth, he became passionate about his own education—working on neighboring farms in Guilford,

1

Connecticut, in order to put himself through the newly formed Guilford Institute, and later Yale College. After a fairly unremarkable four years at Yale, Murray's intensity became focused on his calling as a Congregationalist minister. Starting in rural Connecticut towns, his dedication to the perfection of the sermon, and what he called "old time theology" led to the rapid rise of his fame as a preacher and a blossoming career that culminated at the head of Boston's well-known Park Street Church.

It was his pursuit of fine oratory skill to further his ecumenical leadership that led Murray to begin to write outside of his traditional ministerial duties. To better master his command of the English language, he determined to write on a daily basis. Murray wrote about what began to interest him more than anything else at that time, the Adirondacks and his experiences in that wilderness in upstate New York.

Thus, Murray's drive to become a better minister resulted in the creation of wilderness stories that would become the basis for the book from which he would derive his time-tested fame, *Adventures in the Wilderness*. His passion for the wilderness and advocacy of the many benefits of spending time in nature captivated the urban public of the late nineteenth century and drove thousands to seek the solace of the Adirondack Mountains.

Murray's congregation at Park Street Church was forced to share the attention of its minister not only with the formidable Adirondack Mountains, but also with the horse. Murray loved horses above all other animals. During his successful career in Boston, the preacher earned enough to convert his childhood homestead in Connecticut into a large stock farm for his beloved horses, complete with a race track. Much like his passion for the wilderness, Murray was compelled to write about his theories on breeding horses. These were published in his large volume titled *The Perfect Horse*. The preacher also purchased a patent for what he dubbed the "Murray Wagon" and started a wagon manufacturing company with several investors.

By the mid-1870s, Murray's life was turned upside down in nearly every conceivable manner. His career, personal life, and business interests crumbled, and he fled New England. His tendency toward singleminded obsessiveness and passionate advocacy for his fancies remained intact, though less obvious during this period of his life.

Following his personal crash, Murray's political and philosophical outlook grew quite progressive in nature. Newspaper interviews and lectures reveal a man who appears to have adopted the thinking of the late-nineteenth-century Free Love movement, as an advocate for progressive divorce laws and women's rights. He was, from the beginning, a steadfast and vocal proponent of temperance.

The passion-advocacy spark that drove Murray's life was reinvigorated during the early 1880s. Recently relocated from Montreal, Quebec, to Burlington, Vermont, Murray's eye for natural wonderment and spirit of adventure found a new object to explore and advocate for—Lake Champlain. Like the Adirondacks, Murray introduced Lake Champlain to his readers as a marvel of nature, and pushed for the increased interaction of people with the lake. In this spirit, he became convinced, and sought to convince others, that Lake Champlain was a premier sailing venue. Murray, along with other residents, formed the Lake Champlain Yacht Club and introduced the Sharpie class sailing vessel, a native vessel of Murray's childhood Long Island Sound, to Lake Champlain. As with the wilderness and horses, Murray felt compelled to put his passion for Lake Champlain in writing, and published *Lake Champlain and Its Shores* in 1890.

A subsequent resurgence in his popularity and corresponding success of his lectures, allowed for Murray's return to his childhood home in Guilford. Leaving Burlington behind, Murray moved his wife and two daughters back to his birthplace. There he fathered two more daughters and his final passion. Compelled by strong feelings against the offerings of public education, Murray homeschooled his four daughters and found the results superior. In typical Murray fashion, he would not suffer this discovery of a superior method to go unnoticed. In 1900, Murray published his final book, *How I am Educating My Daughters*. This work, like *Adventures in the Wilderness* and *Lake Champlain and Its Shores*, was an advocacy and how-to book, and in many ways reflected the progressive education reform movement prevalent during that time.

Thus, Murray's passions drove him in various directions during his lifetime, for both good and ill. His tale is one of a myriad of careers, loves, successes, and failures. It is a story of targets hit, near misses, and shots that went wildly astray.

Perhaps more importantly, his often singlemindedness regarding his passions led to effective advocacy. Again and again, Murray became passionate about an object of nature or social movement and then became a strong public advocate for that passion. He found virtues in his passions that he was compelled to share with and preach to the general public.

Certainly this pairing of unrelenting passion and advocacy culminated in the lasting impact Murray has had on the Adirondacks and American attitudes toward nature. Yet, Murray's advocacy of the other objects that captivated him, Lake Champlain, horses, free love, and education, is also important, as it provides us with a written reflection of the social attitudes and changing values in the late nineteenth century and first years of the twentieth. This book explores these passions and the man behind them.

PART ONE

BEGINNINGS

Chapter 1

Guilford

But the old gentleman, so those who knew him say, more dearly loved to sit around with his neighbors and talk than to farm. . . . "He could talk very big too," said a Guilford farmer to-day "and that's where the boy got his gift of talking, and there is no denying that the preacher is very smart in the pulpit."

—*The New York Sun*, August 6, 1879

The story of William Henry Harrison Murray begins in the small town of Guilford, Connecticut. Guilford, located on the shores of the Long Island Sound, traces its history to seventeenth-century America, just before the arrival of the Murray family in the New World. Settled by Puritans in 1639, the town was founded on land purchased from the female chief Chambishi, and the first settlement there was known as Menuncatuck.[1]

Like many similarly founded towns in New England, Guilford grew steadily throughout the eighteenth and nineteenth centuries. On the fertile shores of the Long Island Sound, the primitive initial settlement gave way to a busy agricultural and seafaring town.[2] By the mid-nineteenth century, Guilford had developed a strong farming and shipbuilding heritage.

Not unlike many of the men in the region, W. H. H. Murray's father, Dickinson Murray,[3] reflected this local dichotomy, supporting his young and growing family as both farmer and shipbuilder.[4] In an article published in 1879, *The New York Sun* reported of Dickinson:

Dickinson Murray seems to have been a local character. He could wield a ship's carpenter's adze with the best of them,

7

and there were many coasters that he had a hand in building. When there were no ships to build, the senior Murray did a little farming on a tract of land close by to the now famous Murray Stock Farm.[5]

Dickinson's wife, Sally Munger Murray,[6] had been a schoolteacher before marrying Dickinson in Madison, Connecticut, on April 17, 1831, and joining him at the farmhouse that was even then known as the Murray Homestead. The homestead was a simple saltbox structure in keeping with the rural, New England setting in which it was found. A later newspaper article on Murray described the home as follows:

Mr. Murray occupies the old homestead, where the family have lived for generations. In front of the house are several maple trees, under them chairs and seats for outdoor comfort, and in the garden nearby flowers and monthly roses in full bloom, with a huge button ball tree once a small stick which Mr. Murray's great grandmother had picked up to help her walk, and as she came to the house set it up in the ground, not thinking it would grow, but it took root and stands like a family heirloom, associated with the remembrance of old age and its kindnesses and benediction.

The Murray House is built with the huge chimney in the centre, and the rooms on either side are thrown into one by taking away the doors. On each side are open fireplaces, with bright brass andirons and fenders, when filled with huge burning logs looking more inviting and attractive than stoves, no matter what their shape, or the registers in our city houses, where no bright flame glows with warmth, but through which plenty of gas with noises and voices from all parts of the house ascend to annoy the occupant. About a good many things which we call modern improvements there is considerable question whether they really are improvements. The old-fashioned Venetian blinds adorn and protect the windows of the house, various musical instruments are ready for the touch of skillful fingers, and in the dining-room we see the ancient timepiece that reaches from floor to ceiling, and the ample and commodious side board, so useful convenient that we wonder why that article of furniture should ever go out of fashion.[7]

It was in a small room just off the kitchen on the first floor of the Murray Homestead that William Henry Harrison Murray, who went by Bill for much of his life, entered the world on April 26, 1840. His arrival was preceded by two girls and a boy: Eliza (b. 1833), Sarah (b. 1835), and Chauncey (b. 1837). Bill Murray, the fourth child, and second boy, was followed six years later by Sally's fifth and final child, a girl named Harriet (b. 1846). Similarities appear in the lives of Chauncey and his younger brother Bill, and are worth noting here.

Chauncey Dickinson Murray was born on May 15, 1837, the third child (and first son) of Dickinson and Sally Murray. Like his younger brother, Chauncey pursued a life of ministry and worked to support his education. The eldest Murray son attended the Theology School of Yale College,[8] working as a waiter to earn his board. He was ordained in the Market Street Reformed Church in New York City, and later served as a minister at the Westminster Presbyterian Church on Twenty-Second Street between Fifth and Seventh Avenues of that city. In a step that W. H. H. Murray would echo, Chauncey eventually decided the ministerial life was not for him. He is later said to have practiced as a lawyer and worked at the U.S. Custom House. Notably, while employed at the custom house, Chauncey found a clue to a well-known Bank of England robbery that led to the recovery of $260,000 from a trunk he inspected.[9] He received some popular note, but no monetary reward, for his diligence. Later, Chauncey became a well-known Republican campaign speaker.[10]

~

While the Dickinson Murray family was not strictly poor by the day's standards, it was far from wealthy. Like many families in New England during the period, the Murrays wore homespun clothes and depended on their land and hard work for most of their food stock. According to W. H. H. Murray's lifelong friend, H. J. Griswold, the Murray Homestead was "on the very outskirts of town, which at that time was almost a wilderness. The view from Murray's home was wild and romantic and the woods nearby were filled with squirrels and other game, and the brook which ran at the foot of the home lot was stocked with trout."[11]

Such a setting for his young life likely led Murray to express what would become his trademark dichotomy. As a boy, he was an avid devotee of hunting, fishing, and anything else he could find to do in the outdoors. At the same time, he was both studious and eager to learn.

Murray "learned easily, was a constant reader and early had a reputation as a debater."[12] It is likely that Murray's love of learning, and particularly of reading books, resulted from the influence of his mother Sally. It is not hard to imagine Sally, a former schoolteacher, emphasizing the importance of scholastic study to all of her children. Young Murray's dual dedication to both book and outdoor life certainly foreshadowed the controversy that would arise in his later years when he insisted on the harmonious coexistence of dedication to ministry, outdoor life and, of course, devotion to his beloved horses.

Murray first attended the local public school in Guilford, arriving by foot each morning and departing in the afternoons by the same mode of transportation. It was in that first school that the young Murray apparently stoked the woodstove with gunpowder before the schoolmaster lit the fire, providing a preview of the humorous, if sometimes reckless, traits that he would portray so often in later years. According to his daughter, Ruby Murray Orcutt, this was one of many pranks pulled by Murray during his youth. She wrote that Murray "once set fire to a newspaper held by a beau of his elder sister, Sarah, a wooer far too leisurely to suit my father's notions of how a courtship should proceed."[13]

Murray later joined his friend Griswold at the newly formed Guilford Institute.[14] Guilford resident Sarah Griffing had established the private, coeducational institute in 1855.[15] Murray made the switch to Guilford Institute allegedly of his own accord, undoubtedly with encouragement from Griswold, paying for the tuition through his work on various farms around town, including "cutting the wood, tending fires and working in the garden of a certain wealthy old lady."[16] While the voluntary element of his attendance at Guilford Institute is unconfirmed, it certainly is plausible given Sally's influence when it came to education and the strong sense of curiosity, self-betterment, and ambition that Murray displayed throughout his life.

Griswold tells us that Murray was the most popular boy at Guilford Institute. He was captain of the football team and "planned all of the picnics and excursions into the woods in search of rural knowledge. He was familiar with and could tell where to find the haunts of every living thing, from the smallest insect to a den of black snakes, nor would he wantonly kill or hurt even a snake."[17] Here again, we see Murray's early inclination toward the natural world and the sport it provided.

Chapter 2

Yale

We have a bath room & tub in the first story that we can use any day of the week for a cold bath & can have a warm one whenever we will heat the water.

—Joseph Cook on his rooms at Yale,
in Bascom, *Letters of a Ticonderoga Farmer*

Murray enrolled at Yale College in 1858, becoming a member of the class of 1862.[1] By his own accounts, Murray's entry upon the scene was anything but auspicious. He often told of his arrival on September 5, 1858, at the college wearing clothes made by his mother and older sisters, carrying two carpetbags of belongings of like origin, and having exactly four dollars and sixty-eight cents in his pocket.[2]

Founded in 1701, Yale College was well established by the time Murray entered its compound in New Haven in 1858. The college traced its genesis to a meeting of ten Congregationalist ministers (all graduates of Harvard) in 1700. These founding gentlemen donated books for the purposes of starting a new college to train ministers.[3] Therefore, it is not surprising that the first two hundred years of Yale's history focused on religion and science.

During Murray's years at Yale, the college was led by Theodore Dwight Woolsey,[4] who held the position of president of the college for twenty-five years. At that time, Yale operated on a trimester system, consisting of three terms of fourteen weeks each. Lectures were given three times a day, except on Wednesdays and Sundays, when there were only two lectures. Students attended chapel each morning for prayers and scripture, and attendance at Sunday services was mandatory.

Murray and his lifelong friend H. J. Griswold, along with 132 other young men, were enrolled in Yale's Academical Department.[5] To gain admission to the college, applicants had to be at least fourteen years old and demonstrate proficiency in several subject areas and particular texts. These included Cicero's select orations, Virgil's *Aeneid*, Latin grammar and prose, Greek grammar and prose, English grammar, Xenophon's *Anabasis*, Jeremiah Day's *Introduction to Algebra*, John Playfair's work on Euclid, and geography.[6] According to Yale's 1858 catalog, emphasis was placed on mathematics, because most students were found to be deficient in that area.

The annual costs to attend Yale College in 1858 were estimated to be $215.[7] This included tuition, room, and incidentals of $72; board of $100; and fuel, books, laundry, and miscellaneous expenses of $43. Enrolled students were required to post a bond of at least $200 to cover their expenses.

During his first year at Yale, Murray lived in Room 64 of the South Middle College on Chapel Street.[8] His childhood friend Griswold also roomed at South Middle College, occupying Room 47. As a freshman, Murray was subject to the then-lauded hazing from upperclassmen. However, in an autobiographical sketch, he recalled that he had turned the table on some aggressive sophomores a week into his first year. He wrote: "My health was perfect, I had whirled the flail for six weeks steadily and was sinewy as an Indian, several of the sophomores suddenly discovered that fact when they clinched on to me in the rush in from Union Hall."[9]

While Griswold maintained his room at South Middle College for three out of his four years at Yale, Murray, characteristically, moved around. During his sophomore year, Murray occupied Room 153 of the Athenaeum.[10] The Athenaeum was the last of the colonial buildings at the college and was located on the south side of Connecticut Hall on Chapel Street. The building had originally served as the college's first chapel, but it was converted to residences and classrooms after 1824, following the completion of the second chapel. The Athenaeum's former heaven-directed spire was eventually replaced with an octagonal observatory tower with several telescopes. Murray returned to South Middle College, near Griswold, as a junior and then again relocated to the Athenaeum as a Yale senior.[11]

∾

While studying at Yale, Murray became acquainted with a fellow student who would prove instrumental to his love of the Adirondacks and horses. That young man was Flavius Josephus Cook.

Cook was two years older than Murray, having been born on January 26, 1838, to William and Merrette Cook on their family horse farm, called Cliff Seat, on the edge of the Adirondack wilderness.[12] Cliff Seat was situated in an area known as Trout Brook Valley, just south of Ticonderoga, New York.

Cook was not a fan of his given name, and, as a young man, he quickly decided to go by Joseph. William Cook was determined that his son would make something of himself in the world and devoted much of his life and money to his son's education. Thus, at the prodding of his father, Joseph Cook left Cliff Seat at the age of thirteen in pursuit of education and success.

As a young man, Joseph Cook attended Newton Academy in Shoreham, Vermont, for a short time. He then studied at Whitehall Academy in Whitehall, New York, and finally, Phillips Andover Academy in New Hampshire.[13]

Like Murray, Cook enrolled as a freshman at Yale College in 1858, becoming a member of the class of 1862.[14] Cook, too, was enrolled in the Academical Department at Yale, pursuing his Bachelor of Arts degree.[15] During his first year, Cook lodged at 139 York Street. His many letters home to his parents during this time give us a glimpse of what life was like for young men like Cook and Murray while at Yale. Of his freshman rooms, Cook wrote:

> Our room is a front chamber 20 feet square. . . . Our room
> is lighted with gas. . . . The burner juts out from the wall and
> elbows out. . . . We can shut the elbows back against the wall
> when not burning the gas. We have a wood closet and a clothes
> closet under the garret stairs. . . . All these advantages we have
> for 75 cents a week. I have board in a club directly across the
> street good enough for a king for probably $2.50 a week.[16]

Despite rooming practically next door to each other in the Athenaeum their sophomore year, there is no record indicating that Cook and Murray were anything but acquaintances during their mutual time at Yale. It was not until the two found themselves in Boston years later that their friendship fully developed. Despite this delay of intimacy, there is evidence that Murray knew of Cook and respected him at Yale. Later, when Murray left his church in Meriden, Connecticut, to lead Boston's Park Street Church, he suggested that Cook become the minister at Meriden. Heeding Murray's advice, Orville H. Platt, another close friend of, and important influence on, Murray, called upon Cook to take the position at Meriden. Cook declined.[17]

In 1860, Cook's time at Yale was interrupted by a mental disturbance that the historian Frederick G. Bascom described as "a deranged mind brought on apparently by morbid religious brooding."[18] Whatever the cause of this malady, it resulted in Cook leaving Yale that year. In time, he decided that Harvard was a better fit for him, and Cook graduated from that esteemed institution.[19]

After Harvard, Cook attended Andover Theological Seminary, a Congregational seminary.[20] Though he was never formally ordained as a minister, he spent two years as a substitute minister for churches in East Abingdon, Massachusetts; Middlebury, Vermont; and Malden, Massachusetts. This was followed by further studies at Germany's Leipzig and Heidelberg Universities.[21]

Returning from Europe, Cook eventually established himself in Boston, where he became a popular lecturer[22] and soon earned the moniker of the "Boston Monday Lecturer."[23] Drawing from his education and experiences abroad, he lectured weekly on topics ranging from science to religion to world history.

Again, it was during Cook's time in Boston, rather than at Yale, that he became close friends with Murray. While Cook's home, Cliff Seat, was on the edge of the Adirondacks not far from the shores of Lake George and Lake Champlain, a body of water that Murray would become enamored with later in life, Murray's interest in Cook and his family was more equine in nature.

While Joseph Cook was away studying, his father William had established a notable horse farm at Cliff Seat and bred many Morgan horses there.[24] Murray and his friend Orville H. Platt often camped on Lake George and on the grounds of Fort Ticonderoga on their early Adirondack expeditions. Bascom wrote that Joseph Cook visited Murray and Platt at both places and they, in turn, had spent time visiting Cliff Seat.[25] Murray's interest was no doubt piqued when he saw the horse farm in Trout Brook Valley. Through his friendship with Cook, Murray was eventually able to conduct quite a bit of old-fashioned horse trading with Cook's father at Cliff Seat.

~

On July 31, 1862, Murray graduated from Yale College.[26] In the four years since his matriculation, his class had dwindled in size from the 134 enrolled in 1858 to 98 at graduation.[27] Murray's four years at Yale provided a solid education, but he was by no means an academic star. Unlike Joseph Cook, who won several prizes for English composition and declamation while he attended Yale,[28] Bill Murray's name was absent on the prize lists during any of his four years at the college.

Having obtained his Bachelor of Arts degree, Murray was eager to embark on the next phase of his path to the pulpit. This brought him to a seminary founded in 1834 in East Windsor Hill, Connecticut. However, before he arrived at this next milestone, Murray briefly delayed his departure from New Haven to marry.

Isadora Laura Hull was the second of three children born to Shelden Hull, a farmer, and Nancy J. Booth Hull of East River, Connecticut.[29] She was born in 1845, making her five years younger than Murray. It is not known how Bill Murray met Isadora Hull, but by the summer of 1862, the two were betrothed. Bill and Isadora wed in New Haven, Connecticut, on August 8, 1862.[30]

Chapter 3

Seminary

The creed, which is part of the organic law of the Institution, embodies the old faith of the New England churches, and is grounded, it is believed in the Divine Word.

—Theological Institute of Connecticut,
successor to East Windsor Hill Seminary

Once married, Bill and Isadora Murray moved to East Windsor Hill, Connecticut, a small district within what is now known as the Town of South Windsor. East Windsor Hill lay approximately equidistant, at twelve miles, from Hartford, Connecticut, and Springfield, Massachusetts.

The couple was compelled to relocate to this small town outside of Hartford to enable Murray to continue his studies for the ministry. Murray had enrolled in the East Windsor Hill Seminary in the same year the couple was married, 1862. As he was already a student at Yale, one wonders why Murray did not pursue a course of study at the college's divinity school as his older brother Chauncey had. A resident of Guilford, interviewed by *The New York Sun* in 1879, believed this was a result of a lack of funds: "He had to scrub 'round to make both ends meet . . . but he finally did it and got into the Theological Seminary where there was a better chance for a student who was paying his own way to get through without living on bread and water."[1] While Murray devoted himself to his studies at the seminary, Isadora supported the couple financially through her work as a teacher.

The seminary had its origins in 1833, when a group of Congregational ministers met and formed the Pastoral Union of Connecticut.[2]

These ministers recognized the need for formal ministerial training for New England's Congregational churches. The following year, 1834, saw the establishment of the seminary "on the hill," formally named the Theological Institute of Connecticut.[3] The school stayed at this location until 1865, when it moved to Hartford.[4] Murray's time at the seminary coincided with its last years at East Windsor Hill.

Congregationalism, upon which the young Murray based his future, was part of the family of reformed protestant religions that had their roots in sixteenth-century Europe. The Congregational movement began in England and made its way to America via the seventeenth-century Pilgrims. Notably, Congregational churches had control over the affairs of their own religious community, with no bishop or other external hierarchy. Early Congregational churches in New England were steeped in Calvinist traditions, but as the eighteenth and nineteenth centuries progressed, the Congregational doctrine underwent several schisms and countless adjustments. The old school, Calvinistic traditions that Murray would initially profess to love remained in some Congregational churches, while others exhibited leanings toward Arminianism, Unitarianism, Deism, and even Transcendentalism.[5]

Though the plan must have been for the Murrays to stay in East Windsor Hill until Bill graduated from the institute, that did not happen. For reasons unknown, Murray, like his friend Joseph Cook, did not complete the seminary program. An entry in the *Historical Catalogue of the Theological Institute of Connecticut*, published in 1881, notes only that Murray undertook a partial course at the institute and then lists his subsequent ministerial posts.[6] This early departure is in keeping with an undercurrent of restlessness that appears repeatedly in W. H. H. Murray's life.

THE OLD HOMESTEAD.

The Murray Homestead.

Yale College.

Dickinson and Sally Murray.

Chauncey Murray.

W. H. H. Murray

Isadora Murray.

Chauncey and W. H. H. Murray.

PART TWO

REVEREND

Chapter 4

Pastor

Mr. Murray never lost an opportunity to spend a day gunning on
the hills surrounding the village.

—Harry Radford, *Adirondack Murray*

After his early departure from the seminary in East Windsor, W. H. H.
Murray spent a brief time as a vicar in New York City under Reverend
Doctor Edwin Hatfield.[1] This vicarage, as it was known, was a type of
internship that seminary students often undertook before gaining a
ministerial appointment. While the details of Murray's vicarage remain
unknown, his internship was successful to the extent that it resulted in
the issuance of his ministry license in 1863.

Murray's first pastoral assignment was to a small Congregational
parish in Washington, Connecticut, the hometown of Orville H. Platt,
whom Murray would later befriend while serving in Meriden, Connecticut.
In 1863, Murray became the pastor of the First Congregational Church
in Washington.[2]

In his biographical tribute to his friend, Harry Radford relays a
telling story of Murray's time in Washington and his unique combination
of the outdoor life and ministry:

> One evening he was unusually late in returning. A religious
> service was scheduled to occur that night in the church, and
> the parishioners, as usual, assembled in the edifice, eager, as
> ever, to hear Mr. Murray's beautiful discoursings upon spiritual

subjects. The time set for the commencement of the service arrived, but no preacher appeared. . . . Even displeasure was beginning to be expressed among those whose tempers were the easiest ruffled, at being thus brought from their homes for nothing, when the door of the church burst suddenly open, and in strode the belated preacher, quite heated from hurrying, dressed in his shooting-jacket and velveteen breeches, and carrying in his hand his game-bag and fowling-piece. Without making excuse for his unorthodox garb, or changing the same for ministerial vestments, he quietly hung the game-bag over the back of a convenient chair, leaned the gun against the wall, mounted the pulpit, and opened the service.

Murray's tenure in Washington, Connecticut, was short. He assumed the role of pastor of the Second Congregational Church in Greenwich, Connecticut, in 1864.

~

On April 16, 1865, while at the Greenwich church, Murray delivered an impassioned sermon as the country mourned the death of President Abraham Lincoln, who had been assassinated only two days before. Murray's sermon hit a chord with his congregation, and at the request and encouragement of several men, his words were later published. This was one of several sermons that were subsequently published and contributed to Murray's growing reputation as a preacher. Excerpts from Murray's sermon in the Greenwich church demonstrate both his passion for and growing skill with language:

To-Day the wicked triumph and the good are brought low. Two days ago and the Republic stood erect, strong and reliant, her foot advanced and countenance radiant with hope. To-day she lies prostrate upon the ground, her features stained with the traces of recent grief, and her voice lifted in lamentation,

But, alas! The man we love is gone. The Republic stands as a mother who mourns her eldest son. Others she has as brave, others as wise, others perchance as true, but of them all what one can fill his place?—the one on who she leaned in her first trial, who warded off the blows rained at her by a savage mob when she lay prostrate, who raised her up, builded her a fortress, and at the portal kept evermore his sleepless watch to thwart the throng of Catilines who sought her life, the simple-hearted, faithful man. Who can make good her loss? Well may she be bewildered. The blow came with a suddenness that stunned her. She had not dreamed to dress his bier; her thoughts were on his laurels. She asked not where to bury, but how to crown him.

Nor is he wholly gone. He lives; not in bodily presence, but yet he lives—in the history of his times—in the memory of his age—in the affections of us all. His is a name that will not be forgotten. The living of to-day will tell it to the unborn, and they in turn will repeat it to the remotest age.

Murray's role as minister in Greenwich lasted for approximately two years. In 1866, he was appointed pastor of the Congregational Church in Meriden, Connecticut, and he and Isadora moved to Meriden, where they lived for the next three years.[3] The Meriden church was founded in 1729. At the time of W. H. H. Murray's service there, the church was at the northwest corner of Colony and Church Streets and the building was that congregation's fourth meeting house.[4] During his tenure at the Greenwich and Meriden churches, Murray, by his own account, continued to pursue his three passions in life: old-school theology, the Adirondacks, and horses.[5] It seems likely that his focus on these three passions was honed during these years.

For Murray, at that time, the heart and future of his Congregational parishes lay in adherence to church orthodoxy.[6] This meant severe adherence to the accepted creed. While new-school theologians of the period began to embrace and celebrate a diversity of views, leading many to meld into the relatively new Unitarian movement, old-school theologians like Murray remained convinced that unity under an accepted orthodoxy was the true way forward.

Of orthodox churches, Murray wrote:

Now, friends, this can be truly said concerning the orthodox churches,—they are frank and implicit in the confession of their faith. They deal honestly with the public. They secure no attendance by accommodating men's crotchets. They bid for no patronage by their silence.[7]

A letter from Murray's friend Joseph Cook to his father William gives insight into Murray at Meriden and his inner restlessness:

Last Monday Mr. Murray started for the Saranac Lakes to be absent some six weeks. In his last letter to me he says, "I am beyond doubt, by God's aid, already a power for good in this section of the State, beyond what I had reason to expect, indeed. That I work hard is true, and have for years. For the last few months I have the very delightful feeling that I am at length getting command of myself. My brain no longer okays antics, or goes by jerks and jumps, but is settling down to a steady pace. What I need now is time and health and God's sweet grace."[8]

Meriden was also where Murray met and befriended Orville H. Platt, a fellow Connecticut native. Born in 1827 in Washington, Connecticut, Platt was thirteen years Murray's senior. He came from a wealthier family than Murray and was a graduate of The Gunnery, an elite private school in Litchfield County, Connecticut.[9]

After graduating from The Gunnery, Platt studied law and was admitted to the bar in 1850.[10] He worked for a short while in Towanda, Pennsylvania, and then returned to Connecticut, where he began to practice law in Meriden.[11] Quickly turning his eye from law practice toward politics, Platt became the clerk of the Connecticut State Senate in 1855 and served in that role again in 1856.[12] He advanced rapidly within the state, becoming secretary of the state of Connecticut in 1857 and a member of the State Senate in 1861 and 1862. Platt was a member of the Connecticut House of Representatives in 1864 and served as the leader of that body in 1869.

From statewide office, Platt made the leap to the national political stage, being elected, as a Republican, to the U.S. Senate in 1879.[13] Among his many accomplishments as U.S. Senator, Orville Platt was the author of the 1901 Platt Amendment regarding U.S. relations with Cuba, including the lease of Guantanamo Bay Naval Base on that island that continues today. He served as a U.S. senator until his death on April 21, 1907, at the age of seventy-seven.[14]

When Murray and Platt began their friendship, Platt had already taken many trips with his family and friends into the Adirondack wilderness in upstate New York. Platt was an avid sportsman and was said to have been a particularly skilled fisherman.[15] An early biography of Platt relates a love of the wilderness similar to that developed within Murray:

> Yet, it made little difference to him whether he was lucky in his sport or not. He went fishing for the sake of going, for the pleasure of being in the woods, of building a fire outdoors to cook his primitive meal of bacon and toasted bread and coffee; of loafing under the trees and by the brooks.[16]

Platt established a campsite at Long Lake, on which he built a small, shanty-like structure.[17] The Long Lake camp was extremely isolated, accessible at that time solely by water. It was reportedly a seven-mile row to the nearest post office and an all-day trip by horse to the railroad. Despite, or perhaps because of this isolation, Platt spent much of each summer at his Long Lake retreat until the last year of his life.

Murray accompanied Platt on many treks to the northern wilderness, and Platt later joined excursions organized by Murray. The impact that Platt had on Murray and his love of the Adirondacks is perhaps best reflected in Murray's dedication of his seminal work on the region, *Adventures in the Wilderness*, to his friend.

~

During the Greenwich and Meriden years, Murray made his most numerous treks into the northern wilderness of the Adirondacks. With Isadora by his side, he began to spend much of the summers traveling through the Adirondack forests and paddling on its many lakes and rivers. A report from a Vermont newspaper gives us a glimpse as to the nature of Murray's wilderness trips:

> Rev. W. H. H. Murray and family, with quite a little party of ladies and gentlemen, passed through here Monday en route to the north woods of the Adirondacks via Potsdam. . . . Mr. Murray was dressed in his tourist costume, broad-brimmed light felt hat, blue flannel sailor jacket, leather girdle etc., and was as brown as a nut already.[18]

The Murrays discovered Raquette Lake during this period and formed a base camp there that, for a time, became synonymous with Murray's name. The couple established themselves on one of the larger islands in the lake, then known as Osprey Island, sometimes spelled Ospray. Joel Headley, in his book *The Adirondak*, described the island:

> Ospray Island, lying across the bay, one mile south of Beach and Woods, and half a mile west of Jos. Woods on Ospray Point, contains about thirty acres. This island derived its name from the ospray that yearly builds her nest and rears her young thereon.[19]

At Osprey Island, Murray erected a large enclave of tents. The Murrays named their camp Terrace Lodge, and there the couple entertained many fashionable, well-to-do friends and acquaintances during the summer months of each year.[20]

Murray's friend Radford later wrote of Osprey Island:

> Murray's Island, fortunately, is State land, a portion of the proposed but long delayed Adirondack Park, which, when all its area has been purchased by the State (as it should be at once), will include approximately 3,475,000 acres, and will be the grandest public domain in the world. It was upon this islet that Mr. Murray for many years had his permanent camp known as "Terrace Lodge." Here he frequently found time to compose portions of his earlier books, and from this point, as a centre, he set out upon his numerous excursions into the deeper wilderness. Some persons have attempted to supplant the historic and significant name of Murray's Island (given it in loving recognition and remembrance by the people) with the pretty but far less worthy one of Osprey.[21]

So connected was Murray with Raquette Lake and, specifically, Osprey Island that the island's moniker was indeed effectively changed to "Murray's Island," despite the Murrays having no legal ownership interest in the island. Maps of the period even show Osprey Island renamed as Murray's Island, and this continued into the early part of the twentieth century.

Murray's years-long encampment at Osprey Island led to his testimony being sought in connection with one of several property disputes involving famed Adirondack guide Alvah Dunning. Dunning had claimed to own Osprey Island, or at least a good portion of it, through adverse possession and had sold the land to an unsuspecting gentleman. The State of New York later claimed it was the owner of the island and sued the third party owner to settle the title issue. Murray provided testimony that his camps had occupied the island during 1869 and previous summers, and that Murray knew that Dunning was not on the island during this time as the preacher and guide had had a falling out regarding Murray's claim that Dunning had stolen one of Murray's hounds.[22] The matter went through the New York court system for several years and provides some interesting findings relevant to Murray and the land in question. In a decision filed February 22, 1924, the New York Court of Appeals stated:

> It is now found that one Murray first occupied the island in 1868. Upon it he built an inclosed [sic] camp where he entertained large numbers of tourists, using it for a part of each summer and fall until 1874. Dunning was Murray's guide. He also occupied the camp parts of each year during Murray's absence. Apparently he remained there winters making it his chief camp while trapping. He raised vegetables and there kept his outfit for hunting and trapping but did not claim to own or have exclusive possession of the islands.[23]

These court findings provide a slightly different picture regarding the length of Murray's occupation of Osprey Island than that recounted by Murray, and do not include any mention of the dispute between Murray and Dunning concerning the hound. Murray was sixty-three years old at the time of his recollection of the events that allegedly had occurred some thirty-five years before, and was naturally inclined to add more color to such recollections. The court made its findings fifty-six years after the alleged events, long after Murray and Dunning had departed the scene.

❀

Despite the dual distractions of Platt's wilderness and Cook's horse, addressed later within these pages, Murray's reputation as an up-and-coming preacher grew steadily within New England during his years tending to the Greenwich and Meriden flocks. Word spread of his oratory skills, and Murray's sermons began to be reprinted in several New England newspapers.

Never easily contented, this recognition stoked the fires of Murray's ambitions. In Meriden, Murray determined that to continue to rise within the ranks of preachers, he needed to increase his skills as both a speaker and a writer. To achieve this, Murray convinced himself to undertake a regimen of daily writing.[24] Taking place mostly during the evening hours, when his ministerial duties and outdoor pursuits were completed, Murray began to write about what, at that time, he was most passionate about—the Adirondacks.

These first stories about the Adirondacks focused primarily on Murray's experiences hunting, fishing, and camping in the northern wilderness. Though ostensibly written as private works designed to hone his mastery of the English language, several of these early Adirondack stories found their way into the local newspaper, the *Meriden Recorder*.[25] Undoubtedly, Murray could not help but provide his writings to the paper, reflecting both his constant drive to share his passion with others and his personal ambition.

This local publication was as far as the tales born from Murray's quest to become a better preacher went at that time. It is easy to imagine that the published stories amused many readers even as they bewildered many of Murray's Congregationalist flock who read about their minister's enthusiastic tramps into the godless wilderness. Still, only a few of the stories were published, so the flock's exposure to the conundrum presented by this man of God and outdoor enthusiast was limited—for the time being.

Chapter 5

Park Street: 1869

My friend Murray I had never been able to hear in Boston before; but he spoke this afternoon only some fifteen minutes, and the audience, which numbered about a thousand, was smaller than usual, as no sermon was expected at the communion.

—Joseph Cook, in Bascom, *Letters of a Ticonderoga Farmer*

Boston, Massachusetts, in 1869, was a city in recovery and flux. Its population numbered around 250,000 citizens,[1] but the city had, like many others in the country, experienced great losses during the years of the Civil War. The sense of loss and the scars of the previous years' war was profound among the city dwellers, so much so that a grand musical event was planned that year to lift citizens' spirits and celebrate the end of the War Between the States. The Boston Peace Jubilee was held during the first days of June 1869.[2] An enormous coliseum, also known as the Temple of Peace, was erected in what is now Copley Square. The wooden temple held fifty thousand people and was, though a temporary structure, the largest building in the United States at the time. Featured at the jubilee was a ten thousand voice choir led by Dr. Eben Tourjée, an esteemed man whom we shall hear more about later on.[3]

Along with the Jubilee, 1869 was the year several major city institutions were founded. Boston University[4] was chartered that year, along with the Horace Mann School for the Deaf[5] and the Boston Children's Hospital.[6] Further reflecting the growing progressive spirit within the city, the American Woman Suffrage Association was headquartered in Boston.[7]

Boston also experienced the impacts of the waves of immigrants who landed in America in the latter half of the nineteenth century. Much of the increase in the city's population, despite the war losses, was due to an influx of immigrants. In the decade between 1840 and 1850, for example, the Irish population of Boston increased from four thousand to fifty thousand. Italians, Jews, Russians, and Poles also came to Boston in significant numbers.[8]

These migration waves had a profound effect on the culture, religion, government, and economy of Boston. The once predominately Anglo-Saxon, Protestant city was no longer. As one writer stated:

> Cheap Irish labor transformed Boston from a commercial to an industrial economy, with the native Bostonians reaping the benefits as owners, while low wages left the Irish crowded into the city's first tenements. There were cultural conflicts with the native Bostonians, especially over religion, since the vast majority of the Irish were Roman Catholic, while the Brahmins were Protestant, and politics, since the Irish tended to be labor-oriented Democrats, while the Brahmins tended to be business-oriented Republicans.[9]

As we will see, these were the urban conditions in which Murray would soon find himself in 1869. Such social changes in Boston's culture would come to have a great influence on Murray's ministry, his advocacy for time spent in the wilderness, as well as the man's other progressive tendencies.

~

By the end of the 1860s, Murray's fame as a preacher had spread throughout the Northeast, and his sermons delivered from the Meriden pulpit were regularly published in several New England newspapers.[10] Bill and Isadora Murray were living comfortably, with Murray earning an annual salary of approximately $3,000. Despite ministerial demands, the couple was able to spend considerable time pursuing their mutual zeal for the outdoors.

The comfort that Murray had settled into at Meriden, however, did not last, and, 1869 would prove to be one of the zeniths in Murray's roller coaster–like ride through life. By a letter dated October 9, 1868, Murray had been invited to become the minister of one of the most well-known churches in the United States: Boston's Park Street Church.[11]

Park Street Church was founded in 1809 by a group of twenty-six puritanical men, predominately from the congregation of the Old South Church.[12] Five years earlier, these men had banded together to form a "religious improvement society" in opposition to more liberal strains then appearing within the Congregational ministries. By 1809, the men had established Park Street Church, and in 1810, the growing congregation had raised $100,000 for the erection of the meeting house at the corner of Boston's Park and Tremont Streets. The new church building, which was consecrated on January 10, 1810, was designed by Peter Banner, an Englishman, and constructed on the site of a former granary.[13]

Founded in reaction to the growing Unitarian movement within New England's Congregational ranks, the initial members of Park Street Church were fairly severe in their orthodoxy. They held a puritanical view of the church and its doctrine, forcibly rejecting the more liberal Unitarian doctrine. Its first minister, Edward Dorr Griffin, proclaimed of Park Street Church, "This house, though not raised for controversial discussions, has been built by those who esteem it far from indifferent what doctrine a man believes."[14]

However austere its initial creed, Park Street Church's orthodoxy began to lessen as the nineteenth century progressed. In 1826, abolitionist preacher Edward Beecher took the helm.[15] By the mid- to late 1800s, Park Street Church boasted a congregation of more than nine hundred people, including many influential and wealthy citizens of Boston,[16] and the departure from a traditional doctrine was evident. Even though the strict orthodoxy of its founders had given way to some extent to a more moderate Protestant, social reform mindset, the church prided itself on its quiet, influential, and wealthy stature. This tranquil bliss ended with Murray's arrival.

At the age of twenty-nine, with his evangelical star rising, Murray did not hesitate to accept the invitation to become pastor of the famed Park Street Church. The invitation reportedly came after a three-year search by the church for a new leader.[17] The letter from the church committee promised Murray an annual salary of $5,000 and six months of summer vacation.[18] This was a monumental move up the ladder for the Connecticut preacher, and he and Isadora quickly arranged for their move from Meriden, Connecticut, to Boston, Massachusetts.

Murray arrived in Boston with a substantial reputation as a preacher. He was a popular, imposing figure, and, in many ways, the exact opposite of the congregation that had invited him to become its spiritual leader:

> Fond of fly fishing and fast horses, Murray cut a dashing, and controversial, figure, coursing through the streets of Boston in his racing trap, an expensive cigar clenched in his teeth. . . . Though he caught the attention of the city and filled the pews to overflowing, with the curious from far and near, his own congregation did not welcome their spot in the public limelight.[19]

In his 1968 work *Brimstone Corner, Park Street Church,* H. Crosby Englizian asserted that Murray was "unquestionably the most unique individual ever to pastor Park Street Church. A pioneer and trailblazer at heart, he had no fears or qualms about instituting untried programs and methods even in the sacrosanct headquarters of New England orthodoxy."[20]

Not surprisingly, Murray consciously used his position at the renowned church to further his own objectives. His sermons were widely published, and his fame as a preacher soon expanded beyond New England and the Northeast. The skills he had honed by his late-evening writing exercises in Meriden found purchase in Boston, through his popular, charismatic sermons and lectures. It also led to the other major event for Murray in 1869: his introduction to the Fields, Osgood and Co. publishing house.

~

Founded in 1834 as Ticknor and Fields, the publishing house of Fields, Osgood and Co. was at the height of its success in 1869.[21] In the years since its founding, the publishing house had purchased the *Atlantic Monthly* and the *North American Review,* and it served as the publisher for many well-known authors. Ticknor and Fields's roster of talent was indeed impressive. It included Charles Dickens, Horatio Alger, Ralph Waldo Emerson, Oliver Wendell Holmes, Nathaniel Hawthorne, Harriet Beecher Stowe, Henry David Thoreau, Mark Twain, Henry Wadsworth Longfellow, and John Greenleaf Whittier.

The publisher's offices were initially at the corner of Washington and School Streets in Boston, but by 1864, they had moved to 124 Tremont Street, almost directly across from the Park Street Church.[22] It is no surprise, given this proximity, that the preacher and the publishers crossed paths soon after the new minister arrived at Park Street.

The initial meetings between Murray and publisher James T. Fields are well detailed in Warder H. Cadbury's introduction to the 1970 reprint of *Adventures in the Wilderness,* and no not require detailed recollection here.[23] Cadbury wrote that Murray had ventured across the street to Fields's office and presented his manuscript of Adirondack stories to the publisher. Fields took the writings home to his wife to read. A few days later, Murray was recalled to Fields's office and told "your method of interpreting nature and your humor are unlike anything that we have ever seen. This little book, I am confident, is destined to a great career."[24] Murray and Fields signed a contract to publish *Adventures in the Wilderness,* on February 10, 1869.

~

Thus, by Murray's twenty-ninth birthday on April 26, 1869, the preacher and his wife found themselves in a good place. Murray was the new and celebrated minister of a nationally known church in one of the leading cities of the country. If that were not enough, a famous publishing house had just released his first book, *Adventures in the Wilderness.*

Murray's rapid rise in rank, though, seemed to have taken a toll on the young man. Joseph Cook's correspondence to his father William provides a window into Murray's inner exhaustion and restlessness at this time:

> After the meeting my friend and myself had as much as two hours conversation at his study and while taking supper together at the Parker House. His book on the Adirondacks has just passed into a tenth edition.
>
> I found him very well tired out, as I had expected to do. He told me that he was living in a whirlwind and that if he could have his own way he would drop into total obscurity for ten years, and in that time, rest and ripen for his present work. He repeatedly said, with much emphasis, that he did not like his present life and nothing but a sense of responsibility held him in it.[25]

Chapter 6

Adventures in the Wilderness

> Rev. Mr. Murray, the Pastor of Park Street Church, in Boston, presents in this volume a record of his own camp-life experience in the Adirondacks. He is a practical sportsman, and probably has been more successful with the rod and the gun than any other one of the cloth in the country. His book will be found one of rare freshness and interest.
>
> —Publishing announcement by Fields, Osgood and Co.

It is likely that W. H. H. Murray never anticipated the impact that signing a publishing contract with Fields, Osgood and Co. on a February day in 1869 would have on his life and legacy. Had Murray not met with James Fields and pursued the publishing of his short stories on the great northern wilderness, he would likely have been relegated to a brief footnote in the history of Park Street Church and perhaps New England. *Adventures in the Wilderness* changed everything.

It must be noted, however, that William Henry Harrison Murray was not the first man, or even the first minister, to write of the great Adirondack Mountains. Several volumes had been written about that wilderness before Murray had finished his college education. Nor was Murray's volume the first guidebook to be written about the American wilderness. The earliest guidebook in America appears to have been George M. Davison's *The Fashionable Tour 1825, An Excursion to the Springs, Niagara, Quebec and Boston*, published in 1825.[1]

In 1845, a well-known preacher and author, Dr. John Todd, published his book *Long Lake*.[2] Like Murray, Todd was a Yale man—graduating in 1822—a Congregational minister and a writer. *Long Lake* was Todd's sentimental record of the first settlements of the area immediately surrounding the eponymous lake.[3]

Four years after Todd's work was released upon the public, Reverend Joel T. Headley published *The Adirondak, or Life in the Woods* in 1849.[4] Headley had previously written popular biographies of Napoleon and George Washington. In *The Adirondak*, the author advocated time in the woods as a mental respite and a type of spiritual healing: "An attack on the brain first drove me from the haunts of men to seek mental repose and physical strength in the woods."[5] This is similar to the tone Murray would take in his famed 1869 volume.

Headley's work comprised a collection of letters to a friend, recounting the author's experiences during two summers in the Adirondack wilderness. In the letters, Headley hikes the trails, reaches the peak of Tahawus Mountain; boats on the region's rivers and lakes; and hunts and fishes. In tales that seem to foretell those included in Murray's works, Headley regales his readers with the abundance of fish and game in the northern woods. "Arriving at a clearing, I had hardly swallowed some dinner before I donned my India-rubber leggings and plunged into a splendid stream nearby, after trout. The very first cast I made, I took one, and kept taking them, till, at the end of two hours, I had fifty fine fellows."[6] According to Headley, the deer were as plentiful and as easy to take as the trout.

The theme of nature as the great reviver of body and spirit runs throughout Headley's book. He wrote:

> In the woods the mask that society compels one to wear is cast aside, and the restraints which the thousand eyes and reckless tongues about him fasten on the heart, are thrown off, and the soul rejoices in its liberty and again becomes a child in action.[7]

Headley, like Murray after him, extolled the virtue of the wilderness over that of the city:

> I believe that every man degenerates without frequent communion with nature. . . . A single tree standing alone, and waving all day long its green crown in the summer wind, is to me fuller of meaning and instruction than the crowded mart or gorgeously built town.[8]

The author also attributed divine qualities to the natural experience, declaring that "the good you had forgotten returns, for nature wakes up the dead divinity within you, and rouses the soul to purer, nobler purposes."[9]

One of the more humorous differences between Headley and Murray is their treatment of the pestilent blackfly. While Murray characterized the blackfly as an insignificant nuisance,[10] Headley took a more realistic, but perhaps equally exaggerated, approach to the issue when he wrote that he "was compelled to fling down my rod and run during a blackfly attack for the blood was pouring in rivulets from my neck, face and hands."[11] Headley tells his readers that he has included mention of these flying pests only to ensure that his recounting of the Adirondack experience is an honest one.

Two more notable nineteenth-century men also focused their writings on the wilderness and presaged Murray's works: Henry David Thoreau and Ralph Waldo Emerson. The writings of these famed men predated those of Murray by a decade or more and helped blaze the trail down which Murray would guide his followers.

Thoreau was educated at Harvard University and spent various periods of his life employed as a schoolteacher, surveyor, and editor of a literary magazine.[12] None of these occupations proved to be terribly successful or meaningful to him. While Thoreau never ventured into the Adirondacks, his writings on the power of the wilderness became the center of the natural movement in America decades after they were published. "In his combative and seductive writing, Thoreau gave Americans their first coherent and persuasive conservation philosophy."[13] His most well-known work was *Walden*,[14] first published by Ticknor and Fields in 1854.

Thoreau was a proponent of achieving moral perfection, a state he was convinced could not be found amid nineteenth-century cities, but only in the wilderness. In his own words, Thoreau "went to the woods . . . to live deliberately, to front only the essential facts of life."[15] Natural places were places of spiritual renewal for Thoreau, and his writings insisted that time spent in the forest constituted a proper life while time in the city was only an unwholesome intrusion.[16]

On the Adirondacks, Thoreau acknowledged: "New York has a wilderness within her own borders. And though the sailors of Europe are familiar with the soundings of her Hudson . . . an Indian is still necessary to guide her scientific men through its forests."[17] Content, however, with Walden Pond and the New England forests, he never ventured into New York's vast wilds.

Unlike Thoreau, his mentor Emerson had visited the Adirondacks.[18] Born in Boston in 1803, Emerson too attended Harvard University.[19] He is best known as a leader of the Transcendentalist movement in America.[20] At the core of this movement was the steadfast belief in individualism that itself stemmed from a belief in the basic goodness of individuals and nature.[21] The movement was most popular during the mid-nineteenth century, and it was during this time that Emerson wrote of the importance of nature and the wilderness.

In his 1836 essay titled *Nature*, Emerson "presented the woods as a house of worship without walls" and a place "where boyhood never ends."[22] The transcendentalist wrote, "In the woods, we return to reason and faith. There I feel that nothing can befall me in life; no disgrace, no calamity, which nature cannot repair."[23] Unlike Thoreau, Emerson saw the woods less as an opportunity for reclusive retreat and more a place "to go . . . in good company, and with heyday, and bonbons, and comfort, and gentlemen and ladies, and also with the legs of horses."[24] As for the blackflies, Emerson seems to have appreciated rather than minded such pests, referring to them as "protectors of this superb solitude from tourists."[25]

Emerson's most well-known trek into the Adirondacks was a trip to Follensby Pond in 1858.[26] At that time, he joined nine other prominent men from the Boston area for an adventure that has since been dubbed the Philosophers' Camp.[27] Follensby Pond,[28] between Raquette Falls and Tupper Lake, was named for an English sea captain who secluded himself at the site in the 1820s. The 1858 traveling party was impressive, consisting of Emerson, fellow poet James Russell Lowell, two scientists, two lawyers, artist William James Stillman,[29] and the younger brother of Oliver Wendell Holmes.[30]

The scientists in the group included Louis Agassiz, a Swiss-born professor of zoology and geology at Harvard.[31] Agassiz was world famous, and his participation in the Philosophers' Camp drew much attention to the endeavor.

Stillman organized the trek.[32] He had spent previous time in the great woods and published travel essays of his adventures there in 1855. These essays painted the wilderness as a reprieve from city life, introduced readers to fishing, boating on the Saranac Lakes, and dinner with "Mother J."[33]

This illustrious group from Boston spent a month at Follensby Pond, hunting, fishing, boating, studying the fauna, and exploring the forest. Each of the men, except Stillman, traveled with his own boat and his own guide.[34] The days often ended with campfire seminars given by the participants. It was during these trips that Emerson composed his poem "The Adirondacs":

> All day we swept the lake, searched every cove,
> North from Camp Maple, south to Osprey Bay,
> Watching when the loud dogs should drive in deer,
> Or whipping its rough surface for a trout;
> Or, bathers, diving from the rock at noon;
> Challenging Echo by our guns and cries;
> Or listening to the laughter of the loon[35]

The Philosophers' Camp contributed to the increasingly changing views of the wilderness within nineteenth-century America. As word spread of its exploits, so did the sense that the forests offered inspiration and escape from urban life. Following his time at Follensby, Stillman orchestrated the organization of the Adirondack Club, a more formal endeavor than the Philosophers' Camp, and that group purchased 22,500 acres of land bordering Ampersand Pond near the Saranac Lakes.[36] However, this ambitious effort waned with the approach of the Civil War.

All of these men—Thoreau, Headley, Emerson, Stillman, and their compatriots at Follensby—cut the path that Murray would embark upon beginning in the 1860s and continue down for some four decades. Some, like Thoreau and Emerson, were slow to burn but created powerful, literary and cultural legacies that have endured for nearly two centuries. Murray would soon come on to the scene as a bright, fiery meteor destined to burn out in a matter of years.

~

As we have seen, it was Murray's quest to become a better orator that initially led the young minister to writing. The subject of his daily exercises was the Adirondack Mountains and his fondness for that wilderness. Murray later brought these short stories to Fields & Ticknor in 1869, and the pastor and publishing house subsequently fused them with Murray's unique travel advice, into *Adventures in the Wilderness*.

The book was released in the spring of 1869, and by the end of that summer, it was in its tenth printing. According to its author, *Adventures in the Wilderness* sold at a rate of approximately five hundred copies per week for an extended period.[37] The popularity of the book almost certainly exceeded the expectations of both publisher and author. As one journalist at the time wrote: "It was amusing to see the omnipresence of this book. It seemed to be everywhere. Hawked through the cars; placarded in the steamers; for sale in the most unlooked-for places; by every carpet-bag and bundle lay a tourist's edition of Murray."[38]

On April 10, 1869, the following appeared, together with a lengthy excerpt from the book, on the first page of the *Hartford Courant*: "No book has come to Hartford this year so absolutely certain to sell. Everyone knows who and what Mr. Murray is. He is a muscular Christian, as good a shot and fly-fisher as he is a preacher, and as much at home in the Adirondacks as in his old Meriden parish. Writing upon a subject in which he is perfectly at home he could hardly fail to make a good book, and he has not failed."[39]

The popularity that *Adventures in the Wilderness* enjoyed with the public did not translate into an equally enthusiastic embrace by critics. According to author Terence Young, "the *Overland Monthly* dismissed Murray's writing as 'gorgeous French, badly translated' while *The Nation* found his practical advice to be 'sensible and worth taking.'"[40]

Murray's opus to the Adirondacks consisted of approximately 230 pages and was first published with eight full-page illustrations to accompany the text. The first chapter comprises one-third of the book and is essentially a travel book. This is what ostensibly set Murray apart from other authors that preceded him. Through subchapters such as "What It Costs," "Outfit," "Where to Buy Tackle," "Guides," and "How to Get to the Wilderness," Murray devoted the first part of his book to telling his readers how to have their own adventures in the Adirondack Mountains. While such a how-to style is commonplace today, this was an unusual approach in 1869.

The remaining two-thirds of *Adventures in the Wilderness* consisted of short stories involving the woods, wildlife, and people of the Adirondacks from Murray's unique perspective. These stories were humorous and plainly written. They entertained and encouraged readers to take advantage of the book's assistance to seize their own adventure in the great northern woods. Many of these chapters trace their origin to Murray's writing practice in Meriden, as the author noted in the original introduction to the book. Murray made it clear in these first words of the volume that his intent was to inspire others to discover the value of time in wilderness. He concluded his introduction with the following:

In the hope that what I have written may contribute to the end suggested, and prove a source of pleasure to many who, like myself, were "born of hunter's breed and blood," and who, pent up in narrow offices and narrower studies, weary of the city's din, long for a breath of mountain air and the free life of field and flood, I subscribe myself their friend and brother.[41]

The first edition of *Adventures in the Wilderness* was followed by a special tourist's edition that included a foldout map and more detail on train routes and schedules intended to be useful for those who would follow the Boston preacher into the woods.

Chapter 7

The Rush

The brightest sign of the times is the fact that men and women are beginning to turn their faces toward the country, and in the good old-fashioned way, too.

—W. H. H. Murray, *Lake Champlain and Its Shores*

In the summer of 1869, the Adirondack Mountains were overrun. Thousands of middle-class urbanites from Boston, New York City, and other civilized regions along the East Coast abandoned the comfort of their homes and rushed into the unknown, northern wilderness. These hordes of city dwellers included men, women, and even entire families. They sought a storied wilderness of great restorative and even curative powers. These would-be adventurers were informed by one man, a preacher from Boston. They heeded his words and followed.

Few in the reading public that got their hands on *Adventures in the Wilderness* were satisfied with simply reading about the Adirondacks. Instead, many decided to accept the author's invitation to enter the restorative wilderness themselves. Those readers took advantage of what they saw as the author's detailed instructions on trip preparation, as well as how and where to go once the trappings of civilization were left behind.

So in June 1869, Murray's readers, mostly middle-class urbanites, decided for the first time that a few weeks spent in the wilderness might be not only survivable but also, as he promised, restorative. Their decision marked a seminal moment in the social history of the United States. This was the beginning of not only camping for the masses but also wide acceptance of the concept of the annual vacation. Despite this, the summer of 1869 was in many ways a disaster for the droves of people who went into the wilderness on Murray's recommendation.

The 1869 pilgrimage into the Adirondacks started what became known as the Murray Rush[1] shortly after that first summer and retains that moniker some 150 years later. By today's standards, the Murray Rush seems quite small when the focus is solely on the number of participants. It is estimated that between 2,500 and 5,000 urbanites visited the Adirondacks that first summer of 1869,[2] hardly a populous stampede when viewed from modern times. That number of visitors, though, was tens of times greater than the Adirondacks had the capacity to sustain at the time. There simply were not enough provisioners, guides, or even hotels and boarding houses to service thousands of travelers.[3]

The imbalance between the number of people entering the region and the available facilities and supplies is only partly responsible for the endurance of the Murray Rush within our social history. In addition to the ill-prepared visitors and the disparity of accommodations and outfitters, the weather of the summer of 1869 was quite awful.[4] It was unseasonably cold and rainy. This inclement weather not only prohibited warm rays of sun from reaching newly minted adventurers but also brought indigenous insects out in droves, the most notable of which was the blood thirsty blackfly.[5]

A contemporary commentator provided the following delicious description of a scene that must have been repeated numerous times throughout the summer of 1869:

> Pouring off the trains in hoop skirts and three-piece suits, loaded down with luggage they didn't need and couldn't carry, most were confronted by a handful of dilapidated hotels in the town of Whitehall, on the New York-Vermont border. More importantly, they found dilapidated and completely full hotels. Most hadn't bothered to write ahead for reservations.
>
> At this point, the rookie campers had only reached the entry point to the promised Eden. The goal required two more legs of travel that could take another two days. First, there was the carriage ride over rutted trails too primitive to call roads. Then, there were hours more in low-slung dinghies along waterways that were the only path into the mountains.

There weren't enough carriages or boats to transport them all. The few that existed were booked. Nor could they find guides to tell them how to get to the spots Murray had recommended. Undaunted, many of the visitors hunkered down at this chokepoint. After a week battling black flies, most gave up.[6]

Not surprisingly, many travelers had ill feelings toward Murray and his Adirondacks upon their return home to the cities. These unflattering reports of the "reality" of the wilderness became popular fodder for the press corps, and the early followers of Murray into the Adirondacks began to be labeled "Murray's Fools."[7] The *Toronto Star* commentator explains:

> When they returned home, tired, poorer and none the wiser about Murray's vision of the good life, they were upset. Many blamed the author. Some went so far as to deny there was a storybook wilderness out there at all, since they hadn't seen it. One critic called Murray's guide a "monstrous hoax."[8]

One wonders whether some of the columnists and writers who disparaged Murray and his followers had hidden agendas. For years, wilderness areas such as the Adirondacks had been the exclusive playgrounds of wealthy, sporting men who had the money and time to spend weeks and months in the woods, hunting and fishing.

Murray's writings not only presented the wilderness as accessible and desirable to all men, particularly the newly formed middle class, but also advocated the inclusion of women on such adventures into nature. One writer has asserted that "male aristocratic hunters wrote sarcastic columns accusing Murray of bringing a bunch of carpetbaggers to the Adirondacks and drawing unwanted females into their midst."[9] In his book chronicling the political history of the Adirondack Park, author Frank Graham Jr., concurs, writing: "Sportsman who considered the Adirondacks "theirs" bemoaned the invasion."[10] As an example of this "bemoaning," Graham quotes from an article titled "Abuses of the Backwoods" in *Appleton's Journal*: "We do not consider the wild woods a place for fashionable ladies of the American style; they have, unfortunately, in their education, nothing that makes such places appreciated, and no capability for physical exercise that causes the attempt to be pleasantly possible. . . . Let the ladies keep out of the woods."[11] Words such as these make it easy to imagine the threat that democratization of the wilderness presented to the men who for decades had enjoyed exclusive reign over the wilderness.

One of the most well-known of the women who ventured into the wilderness in the nineteenth century was Kate Field. An actress, author, lecturer, and journalist, Field read *Adventures* in the spring of 1869 and departed for the Adirondacks with three other women on July 4 of that same year. The women dubbed themselves the "Black Fly Club" and camped in the northern wilderness for a month. During this initial Adirondack trip, Field was a guest of Murray at this camp and became a stalwart defender of the reverend. She told the *New York Tribune* that Murray was "the patron saint of the Adirondack Lakes" and that his critics were "far more guilty of exaggeration than he whom they vilify."[12] Predictably, Kate Field's presence in and advocacy for the universal benefits of time in the Adirondacks was harshly met in some quarters. Sportsman Thomas Bangs Thorpe lamented: "And now the wildes . . . have been invaded by Miss Kate Field . . ."[13]

~

Despite the disastrous summer of 1869, the Murray Rush continued for several more seasons.[14] Though overshadowed by the perils of that first summer, Murray's Fools continued to pour into the Adirondack region from 1870 to 1874 with much success. Murray's advocacy of restoration and recreation found a willing ear among the growing middle class of late-nineteenth-century America. The vacation was beginning to be recognized as a necessary part of urban life, and wilderness appreciation was increasingly becoming a marker of social class.

The latter part of the rush into the Adirondack wilderness was aided by new infrastructure. New railroads brought the wilds closer, making it possible to arrive in the Adirondacks within thirty-six hours of leaving either New York City or Boston.[15] Similarly, the continued demands of tourists as they moved in and out of the mountainous region resulted in an increase in hotels, boarding houses, guides, and other services necessary for a successful rest or rigorous adventure in the Adirondacks.

The initial bad feelings from the summer of 1869 survived for some time, and tainted many. But with the success of subsequent years, Murray and his book began to be looked on more favorably. Today, Murray is seen as a "one man chamber of commerce"[16] for the region, and *Adventures in the Wilderness* has been described as the book that "kindled a thousand camp fires and taught a thousand pens how to write of nature."[17]

Eventually, as all things do, the rush into the Adirondacks inspired by Murray dissipated. Murray continued throughout his later life to lecture about the Adirondacks and its importance as a national, if not global, treasure. He advocated the establishment of a vast protective natural park that would include the Adirondacks[18] and never stopped encouraging people to go into the wilderness and take advantage of its restorative powers. Murray was a supporter of the Adirondack Park and an early (1902) member of the Association for the Protection of the Adirondacks. The fervor for wilderness adventure in upstate New York may have ended, but the public's acknowledgment of the significance of the Adirondacks and its desire to visit that wild land did not.

~

A century and a half after the first appearance of *Adventures in the Wilderness*, most of the revelations that Murray outlined in that book are taken as common knowledge. The intrinsic value of nature and the natural world is widely accepted throughout the United States. The importance of rest and relaxation, of the vacation, to working men and women is nearly gospel. These things that Murray pleaded on behalf of and extolled to thousands of people in the late nineteenth century are now part of our collective understanding.

In retrospect, the Murray Rush was successful, and more than 150 years later tourism is a major industry in the Adirondacks. Furthermore, the restorative value of time spent in the wilderness, or indeed any type of vacation, is nearly unquestioned in the twenty-first century. Murray's short stories remain what they always were—fun and creative stories intended to encourage his readers to seek their own adventures in the wilderness.

A deeper analysis of *Adventures in the Wilderness* is beyond the scope of this book. However, one more impact of Murray's book bears mentioning here. As Cadbury noted, *Adventures in the Wilderness* contributed in an important way to the democratization of the nineteenth-century wilderness. Murray presented the Adirondacks, representative of all of nature's wonders, as accessible to men, women, and children of all walks of life. The woods were not to be left to wealthy sportsmen but were to be enjoyed by all citizens. This message is likely Murray's greatest contribution to our culture and one that has endured.

The legacy of *Adventures in the Wilderness* and the Murray Rush is our society's adoption of its basic tenets: the value and importance of the natural world and the vacation. "Murray was among the first to promote camping for camping's sake—not to shoot a deer, not to catch a fish, not to catch up with Jesus, but for the self-evident thrill of it all."[19]

Chapter 8

Park Street: Muscular Christian

We drive out, three miles from the centre of Guilford, over the high range of hills that wall the village, across the valley and its winding river, into the midst of a wild, woody spot to Mr. Murray's farm of three hundred acres.

—"Mr. Murray's Farm"

Murray remained the pastor of Park Street Church for six years, but his popularity within that venerable institution did not last as long. For many conservative members of the congregation it quickly became apparent that Murray and Park Street Church were an ill fit.

While the church was conventional and outwardly quiet, its new minister was anything but. Physically, Murray was a large man, cutting a handsome and imposing figure. Murray's personality, though, dwarfed his physical presence.

Of his preaching during this time, Murray's biographer and friend Harry Radford wrote: "He was in the front rank of great public speakers when Wendell Phillips and Henry Ward Beecher and Sumner and Gough and Brooks set the country on fire with their eloquence, and there are those who listened to every orator of note a generation ago who say he was superior to all."[1] In 1869, Murray was included in an American Literary Bureau advertisement for lecture tour featuring some forty-five speakers including John Hay, Mark Twain, Harriet Beecher Stowe, Elizabeth Cady Stanton, Ralph Waldo Emerson, Susan B. Anthony, Kate Field, Edward Everett Hale, Wendell Phillips, and Henry Ward Beecher.[2] Despite the high esteem Murray began to hold in the public eye, his congregation did not always agree.

The *Daily Observer*, in Utica, New York, explained in late 1869 that "[t]he Rev. Mr. Murray of the Boston Park Street Church is losing favor in his congregation. His Adirondack book rather unsettled his hold on his flock, and his dictatorial ways are not relished by the deacons."[3]

~

Yet it was not Murray's outsized personality or his adventures that caused the most trouble at Park Street; rather, it was his leanings toward elements of populism and progressivism from the pulpit. Murray was not afraid to insist, even to secular audiences, that Boston's Protestant churches had sunk into "a deplorable state of semi-heathenism." In a lecture series given in 1869 across the street from Park Street Church at the Boston Music Hall, Murray urged the well-heeled orthodox attendees to end their "splendid seclusion" and open their doors to all. "Let the wealthiest and the poorest, strongest and weakest, the taught and the untaught, worship side by side," he declared.[4]

Evidently, Murray's beliefs had evolved since he first took the pulpit in Washington, Connecticut. His adherence to strict orthodoxy frayed, and Murray became more progressive in his approach toward God, religion, and his fellow man. According to one history of Park Street Church, "he felt constrained by the aristocratic and intellectual personality of the members of Park Street Church and intensely desired that the church focus on the poor and outcast around them."[5] It is easy to imagine Murray's own humble background coming in to play as he began to advocate for Boston's less fortunate.

Murray took particular issue with the common practice among Boston churches, including Park Street Church, of funding foreign missions to tend to the poor of other lands. He publicly denounced such practices, stating, "I am not so interested in the Christianization of Pekin or Calcutta, as I am for the Christianization of Boston."[6] A letter written in reaction to such statements and published in the New York *Daily Tribune* adds some color:

The Heathen Chinese has found a defender. The Rev. W. H. H. Murray of Boston attempts to show that if we think we are at all superior to the almond-eyed race we are very much mistaken. In the first place, China is old he says. So it is. That conceded he goes on to say how carefully it has kept up its arts and its sciences; how it understood the circulation of the blood 2,300 years ago; how it has an aristocracy of brains. . . . and how it has a religion of pure rationalism, a religion beautiful, humane and active, and ignorant of the power of persecution. Which. is a good deal for a clergyman of Puritan Boston to say. To the enlightened and virtuous people of such a country shall we send American profanity and office-holders . . . ? This is what the Chinese's friend, Mr. Murray, wants to know. The trouble, is, says Mr. Murray, we haven't reduced our religion to practice; what we need is not more ecclesiastical machinery, but more piety.[7]

Further setting himself at odds with his conservative congregation, Murray criticized his deacons for adhering to a loveless orthodoxy and the church for failing to tend to Boston's poor. He openly revolted against the church's pew rental system, in which the benches were rented to individuals and families as a source of revenue:

When "a pew in God's house can be speculated in like a railroad stock, and change three hundred per cent in market value in five years," and "the poor who live and struggle and die within sight of its steeple have not the gospel preached to them," the spiritual problem is obvious.[8]

Moving even farther from the orthodoxy he had originally embraced, Murray wrote:

Let no one dare to preach, under the name of religion, a set of dry, juiceless dogmas to this generation, when men long to hear the glad news of human progress and human redemption. Every chord of my nature harmonizes with this popular note. It is not theology, the science of God, so much as biology, the science of living, that I would impress upon you tonight. . . . A man must be of stunted stock indeed if he cannot grow so as to burst the lacings of any creed man ever devised. Creeds and formulas as the main-springs of Christian activity are of the past; they were born undoubtedly, in part, of the Spirit of God, but also, in part, of the spirit of human bigotry and bitterness and ignorance. The banner over us tonight, under which we are all marshalled, is not emblazoned with the name of Arminius or Calvin or Wesley or Knox; but another name is on it, and the letters of fadeless light illuminate it from staff to border. It is the name by which God is known in heaven and on earth,—LOVE.[9]

Murray's faith had evolved into an active one, and he was determined that practice, rather than orthodoxy, was the future of the church. He preached:

The Church in its internal structure is essentially the same that it was a hundred years ago. It ignores the difference between city and country life, between agricultural sections and great commercial centres, between wants and opportunities of small, thinly populated parish, and the wants and necessities of a densely-crowded metropolis. In its internal organization, in its power to give the public what it wants the Church is an anachronism.[10]

On other occasions, Murray challenged his Park Street congregation to look beyond the mere aesthetics of faith. He sermonized:

Many of you love this church. What for? It will do no hurt for you to analyze and answer that question. You are ambitious. That is right. It is right to be ambitious of others' good and God's glory. You desire that this church shall abide as the fathers founded it. So do I. . . . But I assure you, one and all, that it will not live, and for one I have no desire that it shall live, unless it can live the quickening of public virtue and the salvation of men. Unless you put it in closest alliance with the unfolding and suggestive providences of God in this city; unless you place it in the van of its humanities, its culture, its piety, unless you connect it with the moral necessities of Boston, as a supply connected with the want it meets; unless the poor, destitute, neglected, and sinful shall recognize it as their almoner, their refuge, a fountain of overflowing help and assistance for them,—unless you do this, this church will not live, and it ought not to live. The Almighty does not need ornamental churches here, or famous churches, or churches of noble history and grand conservative traditions, of stately decorum and sluggish, stagnant respectability: he needs churches full of the Holy Ghost, and warm with the fire of a divine zeal; full of holy energies and benevolent activities; full of love and sympathy for the masses, and a wise use of every appliance to reach and elevate them. The church that does the least is the least worth to live.[11]

At the heart of Murray's religious beliefs was action. Along with many other liberal protestant and evangelical leaders of the time, Murray was moving away from a passive belief, focused on eternal salvation, and toward an active practice of the basic tenets of Christ; love and charity. Murray's tendencies were toward that of Muscular Christianity, and this is reflected not only in his preaching and ministerial acts, but also in his advocacy of the wilderness and the vacation. What was Muscular Christianity?

∾

By the middle of the nineteenth century, a slow change was occurring with respect to traditional attitudes toward religion and the wilderness. Much of this change was the result of the pressures that the industrialization of America brought upon its increasingly urban population. Industrialization shifted nineteenth-century Americans from a rural-centered to an urban-centered culture. New factories and manufacturing processes, and the resultant economic and social opportunities, spurred the movement of many from farm to city. The members of affluent society and the new middle class found themselves living in increasingly urban environments with a new type of asset to be managed—leisure time.[12]

Before 1850, leisure time in America had been the province of only the very wealthy: successful merchants in the North and planters in the South. Most of the population had little to no leisure time. Their lives were spent working to survive. To the extent the common people lamented their plight in life, they were comforted by the traditional ethos of hard work cultivated by Protestantism and the promise of just rewards in the afterlife.

Traditional Protestant leaders viewed work as an outward reflection of spiritual grace.[13] The heart of this concept likely stems from the European Calvinist tradition of predestination. Because it was impossible to know who was predestined for hell and who for heaven, Calvinists began to look for outward signs that might reveal who the chosen few were. Hard work and frugality soon became popularized indicators of the so-called elect. Thus, all adherents were attracted to these qualities, and most aspired to some form of attainment of them.

While only a few Protestant branches in America can truly be called Calvinistic, the European Calvinists were the spiritual forefathers of the Puritans who came to America to escape persecution and thus sowed Protestantism in the new land.[14] The values of hard work and frugality flourished throughout early American life and were supported by the religious tenets of this community.

But as industrialization modified the manner in which people lived, a corresponding liberal change began to sweep across Protestantism in America. The liberal forms of Protestantism that began to appear in America in the latter half of the nineteenth century attempted to incorporate modern thought with the traditional tenets of Christianity. Liberal ministers stressed ethics over doctrine and began to enfold elements of science, as well as humanism, into the Protestant faith.[15] This course of thought in many ways was the natural outcome of the ideas and practices of the Enlightenment movement of the previous century.

For liberal Protestant scholars and ministers, the focal point of the Bible became the man Jesus, and, in time, the focal point of Jesus became his ethical examples, rather than his divinity.[16] Jesus's living example was the great moral lesson to be gleaned from the Bible, rather than the more doctrinal elements of scripture. God was gentle and loving, rather than angry and judgmental,[17] and salvation was in abundance.[18] For some liberal Protestants, "achieving salvation was no longer a difficult process since God and Christ were man's friends."[19]

With individual salvation so readily available, ministers and their followers could afford to turn their attention and effort to solving the many social ills plaguing America. Liberal Protestantism encouraged a social Christianity in which it was possible to steadily improve the lot of humanity and strive to create a kingdom of God on Earth.[20] Liberals held fast to the inherent dignity and goodness of men. The sin the liberals sought to address was social sin seemingly tied to the wave of industrialization. Thus, liberal Protestant leaders came to take on the earthly role of social education and guidance, if not outright reform.

With this new focus, Protestant leaders such as Henry Ward Beecher and Horace Bushnell sought to address the problems of the poor and the fledgling middle class in America. Breaking from traditional emphasis on continual hard work and frugality, these preachers crafted sermons to stress the importance of leisure and play. This was not merely a rebellion against tradition, but rather a well thought out response to what were seen as the many maladies brought forth by the twin forces of industrialization and urbanization. Men such as Beecher, the son of a well-known Congregationalist preacher, turned away from "God as punisher" and instead embraced a God of infinite love.[21] The past emphasis on harsh doctrine was replaced with an emphasis on feelings. The social impact of this religious change in view was monumental.

Of particular concern to Beecher, Bushnell, and, later, Murray, was the health of the poor and middle class in the nation's growing cities.[22] With an emphasis on feelings, the liberal Protestant movement found its most accepting audience among the women of the period. However, several ministers wanted to address the troubles of urban men among their flocks; thus, a twist on this new emphasis was required. One of the more successful was known as Muscular Christianity.

The style of Muscular Christianity was developed in the 1850s in America.[23] Men such as Thomas Wentworth Higginson and Edward Everett Hale, both ministers in Boston, adopted this manly take on religion. At its core, Muscular Christianity viewed the health of the body as key to spiritual health. One could not obtain spiritual health if that spirit was housed in a sickly body. Thus, the proper role of such ministers was to address the health of the urban man, both physically and spiritually.

The plight of the health of the urban male in the latter half of the nineteenth century was not a light subject. The rapid growth of cities brought pollution, poor sanitation, and other public health problems to the forefront. Waves of immigrants and poor housing were commonplace in cities such as Boston, New York, and Philadelphia. Diseases such as typhoid, malaria, smallpox, tuberculosis, yellow fever, and cholera thrived in the new urban environments. In one particularly bad outbreak, cholera killed more than five thousand New York City residents during 1849, a year in which the population of that city was approximately five hundred thousand.[24]

In addition to disease, industrialization brought a general condition of nervous exhaustion to many urban men and women. Overwork was seen as a direct cause of nervous breakdowns, loss of bodily power, and premature aging in its urban victims.

Indeed, of the many urban maladies of the late nineteenth century, one of the more prevalent and concerning was a condition commonly known as neurasthenia. Neurotics, the name given to sufferers of this condition, often experienced "local spasms, overwhelming sexual excitement, underwhelming sexual boredom, ticklishness and the cramps."[25] This sickness was most common among the urban middle class and well-to-do and was blamed on the burden of modern life and overwork. Multiple cures were suggested as treatments for neurasthenia, including cold baths, electric shock therapy, consumption of coal tar, drinking extract of cow brains, spas, faith healing, and fasting.

Despite the increase in poor health attributed to industrialization, leisure time was becoming more widely available. With the introduction of increased leisure time to the members of the new American middle class that industrialization brought with it, the question of how such free time should be spent became problematic. Many amusements sprung to life within the bounds of the city to capture the attention of its citizens, particularly its men. These often included whorehouses, gambling joints, and taverns, all things to be avoided, according to the Protestant ministers.[26]

One of the solutions that the early liberal Protestant ministers offered to their congregations was the vacation. The vacation was available to the middle-class members of such congregations, although not the poor. Before 1850, the concept of vacation was known only to a select few in America—primarily Southern planters and wealthy Northern merchants.[27] For these wealthy individuals, the vacation consisted of a mixture of idleness and indulgences. These were the vacations the rich spent in such places as Newport, Rhode Island, and Saratoga Springs, New York.

Beecher, Bushnell, and the other liberal ministers who preceded Murray advocated a less indulgent vacation as a remedy for the ills of the new urban middle class.[28] The proper settings for such leisurely periods were towns or farms, where one could quietly absorb the peacefulness of more natural surroundings. Bushnell himself spent leisurely time in the Adirondacks, often in Keene Valley in Essex County.[29] Activities such as gymnastics and the use of the growing number of public parks were advocated during the rest of the year, when residence in the cities was necessary. All of this was well on its way to informing the new urban society when Murray took the pulpit in the 1860s.

Following in the footsteps of the liberal Protestant forbearers, Murray's theology progressed from a traditional doctrinal view to a more liberal stance. He, like Henry Ward Beecher and Horace Bushnell, focused his ministry in Boston on the physical and spiritual health of his congregation, as well as other urban dwellers. Murray told his flock that "it is not the interpretation, but the application of the Gospel to human affairs that concerns us today. The reduction of Christianity to practice, and not the formulating it into systems—this is what concerns us."[30] To put Christianity in action and address the ills of urban, middle-class men, Murray adopted the approach of Muscular Christianity. His contribution to that movement was the wilderness vacation.

Like many in the Muscular Christianity movement, Murray believed that bodily health was more relevant to the question of spiritual health than doctrinal concepts such as original sin. The Boston preacher recognized no clear distinction among physical, mental, and spiritual health.

For Murray, God was a great "physician" whose most dire cases could be found within the nation's cities. He was "deeply distressed by the impact of disease, crime and the fast pace of city life on the health of all urbanites."[31] Voicing this distress, Murray proclaimed that "the moral position and character of the cities should be considered the question of our day."

The city problem, to Murray, was simple: God had created men, not machines. "God did not make man to act as a piece of machinery held to its course by bolt and screw; he made man for liberty—the liberty of self-action."[32] He went so far as to declare that a blind adherence to the urban routine was akin to "committing slow suicide."[33] Murray told his followers that

> a city life . . . is a grinding life. . . . It wrinkles the face and whitens the head and puts burdens upon man beyond what flesh and blood can bear. It taps and exhausts all the reserved forces of one's nature. It destroys individuals and makes a man to be no more than an ant amid countless number of its kind.[34]

As the minister of Park Street Church, Murray was in a unique position to address the problems of the city—as he saw them. Drawing examples from scripture, he proclaimed to his congregation that "no correct theology could ever come out of convents. The Bible, from beginning to end, is the work of outdoor men. Moses, from the time when his parents put him on the waters in the wicker boat to the time when he passed from the crest of a mountain into heaven, was a child of Nature . . . Adam lived principally in the country."[35]

Typical of the age, Murray addressed these issues in different ways, depending on whether his audience was poor or middle class.[36] For the poor, he prescribed and encouraged vocational education to better prepare men for urban jobs and increase their likelihood to ascend the social ladder. He developed a program to send five hundred orphans to the country to experience the benefits of the rural life. In addition, as we have seen, Murray fought against the traditional buying and selling of pews within Park Street Church, a practice that naturally excluded the poor from participation and thus from being acquainted with "conservative habits and principles" (i.e., hard work and frugality).[37] To Murray, by lifting the poor up into the middle class, the poor would, in turn, be able to avail themselves of leisure time and then the wilderness vacation and other benefits offered by an adherence to Muscular Christianity.

For his middle-class audience, Murray, as assistant to God the physician, prescribed the vacation as the preferred remedy for urban ills.[38] Vacations, according to Murray, allowed men to take back control of the content and pace of their activities, control that many were deprived of in the city. Furthermore, like Beecher and Bushnell, Murray encouraged his listeners to take vacations during the summer months. In the cities, summer was a time of pestilence, when disease flourished, so it was best to remove oneself to the countryside during this time. Avoiding previous calls for passive rural retreats, Murray instead prescribed vigorous activity in primitive settings. As discussed in chapter 6, this was, in essence, a driving force behind the minister's *Adventures in the Wilderness*.

In addition to writing *Adventures in the Wilderness*, Murray devoted many sermons to the subject of vacations. One example included in his published collections contained these words:

> We stand upon the threshold of summer. The pavements begin to burn with heat, and the gutters to assault the nose with noisome smells. We are approaching that season when terror walketh by night and pestilence wasteth at noonday. I exhort all of you who can to get out of the city
>
> You will all make more money in eleven months, if you take one for rest, than by keeping steadily at work during the entire twelve.
>
> I pray you, therefore, friends, take each of you, this year, a vacation. . . . Go to the sea-shore, to the mountains, to the wilderness, go anywhere where you can forget your cares, and cast aside your burdens.[39]

Murray's wilderness vacation combined the concept of activity with the previously passively experienced natural setting. He proclaimed:

> Let the old, old nurse, Nature,—the one mother of us all, who never scolded us when we stole her cherries, never upbraided us when we waded her fish pools and poached on her preserves; the dear old mother than never sickens and never dies,—take you to her bosom again; and you will return to the city happier and healthier for the embrace.[40]

In his view, the wilderness vacation met the urban man's need for a "more healthful as well as a more exciting lifestyle," and he "believed the wilderness to be a liberating environment because it would enable men to recover their childlike capacity for play."[41] For Murray, of course, there was no better venue for this restorative vacation than the Adirondacks of New York State.

~

Echoing his belief in fostering a healthy body, Murray was an advocate for temperance. In fact, Murray's personal experience with the ruinous effects of alcohol led him to a lifelong affinity with the temperance movement within the United States. Joseph Cook explained the basis of this affinity in a letter to his father: "Murray spoke to me, for the first time in his life, of intemperance as one of the public evils he resisted from an agonizing personal experience in regard to his own father, who does not now live with his mother and is intemperate."[42] The familial history behind Murray's temperance advocacy was made clear in a sermon delivered by the minister in 1874:

> You are talking like silly idiots when you say there is no danger in the cup. I know from the blood of five generations of cider drinking ancestors in my veins, the danger there is in this thing . . . that abstinence is the only safe course to pursue.[43]

Driven by his father's struggle with alcohol, Murray took firm stances in favor of temperance from the very earliest days of his work as a minister. He delivered a powerful sermon outlining the arguments for temperance as against those for license on April 28, 1867, at his church in Meriden, Connecticut. In that sermon, later published as "Prohibition vs. License" by his congregation and the Massachusetts Temperance Alliance, Murray proclaimed:

> To say that that which bewilders and confuses can make lucid and clear; which exhilarates with an unnatural energy or stupe-fies like a deadly narcotic; which impoverishes when wealth is needed; which cuts the sinews of industry; imperils commerce and breaks the wheel of manufacture; which makes gross and imbrutes the soul; which presses a man down into the gutter and filth of intellectual, social, and spiritual degradation; to say that this has been the basis and the chief agent of the world's progressive movement is to reach the climax of audacious assertion and suggest doubts as to the sanity of the speaker.[44]

Murray made it clear through his preaching that imbibers of lesser poisons such as wine and beer were not the immediate target of his push for temperance. Rather, Murray, like many of the period, targeted "the fatal production of the still; that we seek to protect the masses and ourselves not from the drinking customs of the ancients, but from the drinking customs of the moderns; not from the classic beverages of Greece and the mild liquors of Italy, but from poison the most intense, from adulter-ations the most fatal, and customs which are growing to be yearly more disastrous."[45] The preacher stood firmly opposed to gin, rum, whiskey, and brandy and the "rumocracy" that threatened to ruin America.[46] That prejudice in favor of wine though seemed to wane in later years, for Mur-ray later told congregations that "there is not a person here, I presume, who would stab a man: yet there are men here into whose side you had better drive a knife, and let life out forever, than to offer a glass of wine; for, should they drink, out of them would go what is sweeter and nobler than life,—hope, and love, and fealty to virtue."[47]

Like many in the temperance movement, Murray saw the cause as one that benefited society as a whole, and not just individuals. He told his audiences that the "movement has been for its widest object not the benefit of the individual few, but the reformation of the whole country."[48] He believed that the temperance movements within the nation's cities would carry the movement forward and spread throughout the country.[49]

Murray did not confine his temperance advocacy to the pulpit. In 1873, he was among the petitioners to Boston's Board of Alderman seeking the enforcement of the prohibition of the manufacture and sale of liquor within the city, a law that had been adopted in that seminal year of 1869 but not enforced.[50] The minister also organized and held regular temperance meetings at Park Street Church,[51] and gave temperance lectures during which he advocated amending the United States Constitution to prohibit the sale and use of alcohol, holding that liquor in particular was "destructive of manhood and contrary to the safety of the republic."[52]

A 1917 letter to *The Sun*'s editor regarding the steamer *John Romer*, a steamship serving Manhattan and Long Island and owned by William Marcy Tweed, boss of Tammany Hall,[53] included this story of Murray, while he was employed at the Congregational Church in Greenwich, Connecticut:

> He was a strong advocate of temperance. He rejoiced in the new steamboat, but when he was told that a bar was to be maintained aboard he predicted the failure of the enterprise. Some of the officers were prominent members of his church, who would have perhaps have kept the bar out had their stock holdings been sufficiently large. When the bar had become a certainty, the Rev. Mr. Murray devoted a morning sermon to the sin of the bar, mentioning the fact that an attempt had been made to console him by the fact that the location of the bar was "out of sight, way down below," which he said was the "exact location of hell."[54]

Murray's involvement in the temperance movement is consistent with both progressive and evangelical movements that were increasingly prevalent in cities such as Boston in the nineteenth century. New England was indeed a leader in the movement to reduce, if not eliminate, America's intake of alcohol. The co-publisher of Murray's 1867 "Prohibition vs. License" sermon, the Massachusetts Temperance Alliance had been founded in Massachusetts as the Massachusetts Society for Suppression of Intemperance in 1813. Later, in 1826, the American Temperance Society was founded in Boston. Thus, while understandably driven by his father's alcoholism and its impact on his family, Murray's participation in the temperance movement was consistent with his overall evolution from "old school theocracy" to a more progressive approach to religion and social reform. His stance against alcohol was a natural fit with his endorsement of Muscular Christianity and the strong connection between physical and spiritual health.

～

While Murray's beliefs seemed to be quickly evolving, those of his congregation at Park Street were not. Thus, the six years Murray spent as spiritual leader of the Park Street congregation were fraught with nearly constant turmoil, with Murray leaning increasingly toward progressive causes while his congregation remained more generally conservative. Although the invitation to Murray from Park Street Church in 1869 was greeted by both parties with enthusiasm, and certainly changed both Murray's life and the church permanently, historian H. Crosby Englizian wrote, "Not many months had passed by before the congregation began to realize that their new pastor was not of common mold. As a realist and an innovator he began early to introduce ideas and methods which were novel to Park Street Church. These tended to create a hostile sentiment which was destined to grow to large proportions in six years."[55]

Still, the turmoil he fostered within Park Street Church did not veer Murray's star from its meteoric course. Murray's sermons at Park Street were increasingly popular, just not with the church's traditional congregation. "His church has been lifted to a level of near-universal observation," a popular magazine raved, adding, "Murray's influence is beyond calculation."[56]

～

On the whole, the Murrays appeared to settle into Boston life quite well. Their adaptation to urban life was, with little doubt, made easier by the large increase in annual income that came with the Park Street Church job. Bill and Isadora Murray were living more than comfortably on his $5,000 annual salary[57] and enjoying the attention the reverend's position brought. Beginning in the spring of 1869, in addition to the church salary, the couple began to realize substantial revenue from the sales of *Adventures in the Wilderness* and Murray's lectures based on that volume. Interestingly, Murray later credited these lectures, more than the book, for his success in bringing attention to the Adirondacks.[58] The lectures, which Murray delivered some five hundred times between 1869 and 1872, proved to be lucrative. Each lecture earned Murray between $100 and $250.[59]

In addition to his wilderness-inspired talks, Murray lectured on topics more closely related to his profession as clergyman. While at Park Street Church, the pastor found time to publicly attack a cherished church tradition: deacons. He "lambasted Park Street deacons for their dry, love-less orthodoxy."[60] Murray developed a lecture titled "Deacons" to express his concern over the troubled institution and delivered that lecture to audiences four hundred times in four years. The four hundredth lecture was delivered at the Boston Music Hall. In his own words, "the lecture on 'Deacons' cured a growing evil in the Congregational Church and literally, in many places revolutionized its management."[61]

Murray later published his "Deacons" lecture in book format. In his introduction to this work, the author wrote: "The lecture was written to call attention of the Church and people to the perversion and abuse of an office in our Congregational churches which was created to assist the pastors by relieving them from much of the detail work of the parish, that they may give their thoughts more entirely to the preaching of the Word; but which through certain causes, today fulfills no such service."[62] The author included a list of types of deacons he and churchgoers often encountered: the generally bigoted, narrow-minded deacon, the querulous deacon, the heresy-hunting deacon, the timid deacon, and, of course, the old-fogy deacon. The bulk of Murray's "Deacons" focuses, pointedly and humorously, on three deacons; Deacon Slowup, senior deacon of the First Congregational Church of Fossilville, Deacon Sharpface, whom Murray describes as harsh, unloving, and wickedly cunning, and the much admired Deacon Goodheart.[63] The author obviously did not hesitate in expressing his feelings toward those who held the deacon title, and made sure to drive his point home to listeners and readers:

> But, although the "esquire" and "parson" have passed away, the "deacon" still lives; not as a class but here and there as a remnant, an exception, we will say. Almost every church has one or more who represent the reverse of progress, of fitness for the office, of humility, of charity.[64]

Chapter 9

The Perfect Horse

> If a minister can teach men how to do it, it is not abandoning his profession, but pursuing a remote department of it, which has too long already been left to men who look upon the horse as an instrument chiefly of gambling gains or of mere physical pleasure.
>
> —Henry Ward Beecher, qtd. in *The Perfect Horse*

The money Murray earned from his lectures, together with book sales, brought an annual average of $10,000[1] in additional income to Bill and Isadora Murray during a time when the average American annual household income was approximately $1,400.[2] In today's money, the couple was living on an annual sum of approximately a quarter of a million dollars.

While his annual income was large, Murray found little difficulty spending most of what he earned. A vast amount of his expenditures centered upon horses, which surely displeased the conservative members of his congregation. In 1870, Murray purchased the old Murray Homestead in Guilford and two adjacent farms to establish a thoroughbred horse farm.[3] Thoroughbred horses are known for their agility and speed and are bred for racing. This breed of horse began in the seventeenth century, when mares native to England were crossbred with Arabian stallions.[4] Even today, all thoroughbred horses can trace their lineage back to one of three Arabian stallions.[5] Despite this common understanding of the term, Murray, in typical fashion, developed his own definition of thoroughbred horses. For him, the term *thoroughbred* signified "certain indispensable qualities which give value to the animal and decide his rank and place in the grade to which he belongs. Among these may be mentioned beauty of form, toughness of bone and muscular structure, vivacity and docility of temperament, intelligence, and above all, perhaps in value, the *power of endurance, and the desire to do.*"[6]

Influenced by William and Joseph Cook, Murray had long been infatuated with the equine, particularly Morgan horses. In purchasing the homestead and surrounding farmlands, his aim was to create and operate a world-class thoroughbred breeding farm. Joseph Cook wrote his father William about Murray's purchase in the fall of 1870, "my friend has bought the old homestead in Guilford, where he was born and is putting stock on it."[7] In this effort, Murray was quite successful.

Investing approximately $50,000, Murray combined two neighboring farms with the homestead land to create a large horse farm that he named Murray's Stock Farm.[8] The farm encompassed some three hundred acres, and its headquarters was established within the Charles Frances House, just down the road from the original Murray Homestead. Behind the headquarters, on land from the same farm, Murray had a racetrack constructed. A windmill was installed on the property to provide water to the horses, and several large barns, with horse stalls, were erected. Ida E. Hull, Isadora Murray's sister, was placed in charge of the stock farm and served for ten years as its superintendent and bookkeeper.[9] The preacher and author entertained many guests at his stock farm and clearly took great pride in the property and his horses. The *Hartford Daily Courant* describes such a scene:

> W. H. H. Murray, pastor of the Park Street Church in Boston, entertained a select party of Boston friends at his country home in Guilford Saturday. Among them were Governor Ingersoll, ex-Governors Claflin and Stewart J. Hyatt Smith of New York, and several journalists. Mr. Murray displayed his thirty-three fine horses.[10]

The following article, published in the November 28, 1874, edition of the *Baltimore Sun*, provides a vivid rendering of the stock farm:

> In this pleasant seaside town, the Rev. W. H. H. Murray, the popular Boston preacher, has his country home. We drive out, three miles from the centre of Guilford, over the high range of hills that wall the village, across the valley and its winding

river, into the midst of a wild, woody spot to Mr. Murray's farm of three hundred acres. On the place are five large barns and a sixth is in process of erection, with three or four farm houses. The open fields are divided into cultivated lots, each one numbered and the numbers marked on white signboards, so that the farming preacher from his Boston home can send various directions as to what shall be done with this or that lot on the Guilford farm. . . .

In some handsome, smooth lots on the edge of the woods, Mr. Murray has made a race course a half mile in extent, where his fast horses can be exercised and trained. In the centre is the judges' stand and from it we can view the country for long distances in various directions. . . .

This is the preacher's recreation. In farming and training horses, to develop strength of sinew and muscle, with plenty of brain work to develop intellectual power. He has no less than forty colts and horses, and blooded and thoroughbred trotters and those trained to run, each with some special value. From the large barns flags are flying with the names of the horses upon them, as Live Oak, Morgan Abdallah, Star of the South, Flying Bell, Galuare, etc. Here you are shown a favorite, the young Adirondack colt that came from Ticonderoga, New York, another, Fanny Drew, a two-twenty trotter, Star Abdallah, or the Pride of Guilford. Black Bess, Gypsy, Beauty, Pet, Messenger and many others. There are several grooms who have charge of the horses, and give them faithful care. A shelf of medicine is at hand, in the grooms' office; horseshoes hang up, harness and saddles, with sulkies, trotting gigs, and vehicles of various sorts, everything that horse or rider needs stand ready for use.

The walls of the large carriage-house are adorned with pictures, in which the animal kingdom is well represented in famous horses, Audubon's curious birds, his pictures of wild turkeys and ducks, the frigate bird, dogs, flowers, the village blacksmith and a picture of Mr. Murray himself, and on each side of the entrance are stag's heads, with their beautiful antlers, one killed in the Adirondacks, the other killed in the Murray deer park. Nearby are the dog kennels, where we see ten little black and white pointers, then a Brazilian squirrel in its cage, a fish pond filled with goldfish, a trout pond with plenty of trout, and beyond the fish pond the deer park on a rocky ledge, with a grove of trees, where the deer bound from rock to rock as if in their native woods.[11]

That Murray was a lover of all things equine and devoted large sums of money to the pursuit of that love is without doubt. In the nineteenth century, this devotion was nearly as well known as Murray's passion for the outdoors, and, though not as popular as "Adirondack Murray," the moniker "William Horse Murray" was often applied to the preacher.

$\sim$

If there were any doubts of his great admiration of horses, Murray put those to rest in 1873 by way of *The Perfect Horse*,[12] his guide to the breeding and training of horses. That the minister of the lofty Park Street Church would concern himself with such things as the temperaments and rumps of various horses, let alone discuss the qualities of their semen, was sure to raise more than a few eyebrows. In an apparent attempt to get ahead of the anticipated criticism, Murray was able to convince his friend and fellow preacher Henry Ward Beecher to write an introduction to the work. In addition, Murray dedicated his volume to President Ulysses S. Grant, who Murray stressed was a fellow "lover of the horse."[13]

Within the pages of *The Perfect Horse*, Murray outlined his philosophy of horse breeding and training. In the preface, he wrote: "I purpose in this volume to treat of the most noble and useful of domestic animals— the horse. The book contains many illustrations, as well as chapters on breeding, sires, dams, training a colt, how to shoe a horse, the Morgan horse, and agriculture and the horse."

Amid the technical discussions within *The Perfect Horse*, several passages provide insight into the depth of love and respect that Murray had for his subject. He wrote in the preface:

> If any should express surprise that one in my profession should devote his leisure to such a purpose I have this to say, That to me it has been a labor of love in the first place for the noble animal of which I write, and whose existence and services have even been and are to-day closely connected with the commercial, social and religious development of the country; and, in the second place, I acknowledge the presence in my heart of

a desire to associate myself in every honorable way with that class of my countrymen, to which, by birth, early education, and present aspiration, I belong—the agricultural class.[14]

Later in the book, Murray expounded on the topic:

In short, everything that loving ingenuity can devise should be done to impress upon his mind this early in life that man is his natural protector and friend, and between whom and him an intimate companionship has been ordained by beneficent Nature, which insures that he shall be protected and cherished while he serves. . . .

The horse has a *heart*-claim upon us. The young colt is, in some sense, a member of the family, and one of the owner's household, second in rank and dignity only to the children. . . .

Kindness to animals is, as I understand it, therefore, a duty, an obligation resting on everyone with the force of a moral injunction.[15]

The critical reception of Murray's volume on the horse was generally cold. *The Worchester Spy* concluded:

The whole volume is a mistake. As a guide to the inquiring, it is lamentably weak; it is padded into a diffuseness that makes it wearisome and its enthusiasm about nothing is so amateurish, that by for the occurrence of opinions quoted from real authorities, the whole affair would seem a joke. The key note of the book, running through every page, is indiscriminate praise of the Morgan breed of horses.[16]

The *Daily Graphic* in New York was kinder in its review of the subject matter of *The Perfect Horse*, but it did not miss an opportunity to take a shot at its author:

Parson Murray's book on the "Perfect Horse" attracts a good deal of attention, and is probably the best book we have on that subject. Some of the superfine religionists object to a clergyman's writing a book on such a secular subject, but most readers will be likely to see as much religion in the Perfect Horse as in the

Beast of the Apocalypse or the Dragon with seven heads and ten horns. Every man should write on the subject he is most familiar with and Parson Murray is evidently more at home on the Perfect Horse than on theology.[17]

The Perfect Horse is another example of Murray's absolute dedication to a passion and his desire to preach that passion to the masses. In his Author's Preface to the work, he writes: "I desire to put into a small compass and cheap form the result of many years of reading and observation, that every farmer's boy in New England may have in his possession a book which shall contain within its covers enough of instruction to qualify him to breed, train and drive, buy and sell horses intelligently and profitably."[18] The critics at The Worchester Spy had not exaggerated, though, as Murray, as always, was not shy in expressing his opinion as to which horse breed was superior. At the end of the book, Murray devotes an entire chapter espousing the virtues of his preferred breed of horse, the Morgan. He tells his readers over and over again that "the family of horses which has been distinguished by, and embodied, the four great essentials of the perfect horse,—beauty, docility, endurance, and speed,—is the Morgan."[19]

Murray believed that his passion and love for horses, particularly Morgan horses, was worthy enough to be shared with the public and pressed upon them. The Perfect Horse is not only his ode to that beloved animal but a detailed 'how to" manual similar to Adventures in the Wilderness, and later, as we shall see, Lake Champlain and its Shores.

Chapter 10

Park Street: Separation

No greater mistake can be made than to suppose that Christianity is a creed. Intellectual belief, however correct and biblical, is not piety. Christianity is a principle and not a faith.

—W. H. H. Murray, *Words Fitly Spoken*

As Murray divided his time among his stock farm, Adirondacks lectures, and ministry at Park Street Church, the city of Boston continued to evolve, affected by both local and national events. Notable among these were a great fire and a great depression.

On November 9, 1872, at around 7:30 pm, flames erupted in the basement of a warehouse on Boston's Summer Street. Thus began the largest fire in the city's history. During its twelve-hour life, the Great Fire of 1872 consumed some sixty-five acres of downtown Boston, including the city's financial district. While only thirteen people died, including two firemen, due to the fire, the property loss was massive. More than seven hundred buildings were destroyed.[1] The fire came within two blocks of the Park Street Church, but no closer.

The Boston fire was a powerful blow to the city's economy. The widespread destruction left an estimated one thousand people homeless and some twenty thousand workers without jobs, adding countless families to the list of the city's poor.[2]

Little more than a year after the Boston fire, a national crisis struck. On September 18, 1873, the banking firm of Jay Cooke and Company declared its insolvency.[3] The Cooke firm was followed by several other financial concerns on Wall Street, setting off what became known as the Panic of 1873 that then bled into the Long Depression for the rest of the decade.

Amongst this tumult, Murray's progressive messages hit home among the liberally bent and the increasing number of urban poor to whom he wanted to extend his ministry. Of Murray during this time, Joseph Cook wrote:

> I have seen Mr. Murray, took dinner with him at the Parker House by his invitation, and afterwards conversed with him three hours in his study. My impressions are that his heart is sound; and that, in spite of a constant whizzing of criticisms and attacks from cultured sources in Boston, his general hold upon the middle class of culture here has strengthened in the last two years.
>
> The fact that Boston hears him preach makes his book on the horse seem other than the best half of him. I think that the book, however, has perhaps this far injured his influence. A new edition of it is to appear soon and I will send copy to my father. Mr M. has had a slight paralytic shock and talks of taking a year's rest. He remembers my father with much affection; and I found he knew more of my father's horses, including the one now in law, than I do.[4]

In 1873, W. H. H. Murray's father, Dickinson Murray, died. This prompted another typical Murray move that raised eyebrows[5]—he presided over his father's funeral. The *Christian Union* wrote: "The Rev. W. H. H. Murray, of Boston, in officiating at the funeral of his father, certainly violated a conventional rule; but who shall say he violated any law of inherent propriety, or that he did not set an example that in many circumstances might by wisely imitated? . . . We can imagine a case in which a son might well shrink from officiating at his father's funeral; but in many instances we should think such a service on the part of a son would be peculiarly appropriate and beautiful."[6]

Despite his large public following, the strained relationship between Murray and the more conservative members of the Park Street congregation came to a breaking point in the latter part of 1873. At this time, Murray began to hint of his desire for the appointment of an assistant minister at Park Street to aid him in tending to his flock.[7]

In March 1874, Murray dropped any pretenses he might have had and made it clear to his congregation that he wanted to have an associate minister appointed.[8] Such a minister would share the burden that Murray bore—principally, in Murray's view, that of tending to the flock. The appointment of an assistant minister would leave Murray free to lecture and preach, tasks toward which he was much more inclined.

On April 10, 1874, *The New York World* printed the following:

> Rev. W. H. H. Murray has addressed a letter to the Committee of Park Street Church and Society giving Scripture and other reasons why he should have an associate in his pastoral labors. He says if a lack of funds stands in the way it will be an actual pleasure for him to assist the organization is this direction. He therefore proposes to the church and parish, in case they call an associate pastor, to surrender his present salary to the treasure of the parish until such time as the income to it shall so far exceed the annual expenses that they feel at liberty to renew it or such portion of it as may seem to them needful and proper. . . . The Committee of the Church have the subject of the communication under consideration.[9]

A special committee to take up the question of an assistant minister was formed in response to Murray's demands. On April 29, 1874, the committee made two presentations, constituting majority and minority opinions on the matter, held before a special meeting of the congregation.[10] The majority opinion supported Murray and was in favor of hiring an assistant minister. The minority opinion was against the associate minister concept.[11] The official minority opinion stated:

> It has not been claimed that Mr. Murray has exhausted his strength in his labors with and for Park Street Church and yet it is asked that Park Street Church should furnish assistance in performing the duties which have not exhausted Mr. Murray's strength.[12]

The congregation members in attendance at this special meeting of the church voted sixty-four to thirty-four in favor of the majority report.[13] Following the vote, a search committee was formed and charged with finding a suitable assistant minister for Murray.

Even if Murray's absences could be tolerated, the doings of the Park Street Church minister during such absences were of utmost concern to the church elders. Many of the conservative church members had come to terms with their pastor's love of outdoor life and advocacy of the virtues of the wilderness. What they likely could not tolerate was Murray's passion for horses, horse racing, and the gambling that seemed to naturally follow such pursuits. This was probably too much for even the most liberal of the church elders.

On March 26, 1874, Cook wrote to his father about the situation at Park Street Church:

> After the newspaper gale produced by the criticisms made on Murray in his church, I saw him and Deacon Farnsworth separately. Murray was evidently annoyed, but in good spirits; and the Deacon said that he had received any number of letters endorsing his remarks as printed in the newspapers. There are two parties in the church and Murray thinks his side is much the stronger. I hope the difficulties will be settled; but I should not be surprised if Park St. had another pastor during two or three years. Probably Murray has been careless; he has visited little; his farm and his lectures take time his people ought to have; but his sermons everyone seems to consider excellent. He knows very well that I think he makes too much of horses. Heaven to me will be perfect, even if it does not contain a racecourse.[14]

Cook's words to his father proved prophetic. Despite the formation of a search committee for an assistant minister, it appears that there was little progress in the endeavor by the fall of 1874. Finally, fed up with the failure of the church to staff the position, Murray submitted his letter of resignation on October 11, 1874.[15]

Murray announced the resignation publicly by reading the letter to his congregation, "tendering his resignation as their pastor and asking that it be accepted, to take effect on November 12, at the sixth anniversary of his pastorate. The reason he gave for this resignation is the failure of the church to provide an assistant for him, and, secondly, the extended boundaries of the parish."[16]

Thus, W. H. H. Murray's six-year ministry at Park Street Church ended. According to Englizian: "Murray was in many ways a good and well-meaning man, yet he failed to avoid the pitfalls of a young, gifted and popular preacher. He failed to balance zeal with wisdom and prudence, and to discipline himself to perform the required duties of the pastoral office."[17]

Chapter 11

Boston Music Hall

Rev. W. H. H. Murray is in trouble.

—*Danville* (Vermont) *North Star*, Aug. 8, 1879

Murray's departure from Park Street Church in November 1874 did not bring an end to his ministry. Throughout much of his tenure at Park Street, Murray had held extraneous services on Saturday evenings at the Boston Music Hall on Winter Street.[1] These Saturday evening events were increasingly popular during the years leading up to 1874. One reason certainly must have been that the larger music hall comfortably accommodated many more people than the nearby church, and those wishing to hear Murray's sermons could do so while sitting, rather than enduring the standing room–only ordeal that Sunday services at Park Street Church often presented during this period.

The Boston Music Hall was built in 1852 on Winter Street, just off of Tremont Street and a short walk from the Boston Common,[2] and had an additional entrance off Hamilton Street. The hall was the original home of the Boston Symphony Orchestra, though the symphony's use of the building did not begin until 1881. In addition to being a music venue, the hall enjoyed a long history as a venue for lectures, including many abolitionist gatherings. On the eve of President Lincoln's Emancipation Proclamation effective date, Frederick Douglass, Wendell Phillips, Harriet Beecher Stowe, William Lloyd Garrison, and Harriet Tubman were all gathered in the hall to celebrate the momentous occasion.[3] In the late 1850s, Henry Morgan, the famed "Poor Man's Preacher" had filled the Music

Hall on many occasions to "present the gospel to the working-classes."[4] Murray, then, was in good spiritual stead when he chose to establish his independent church and continue his ministry at the hall in late 1874.

A *New York Herald* article sheds some light on the grand scheme of Murray's new Music Hall Independent Congregational Church:

> Bostonians, or those of them who are progressive and modern in the theological and literary tastes, are now rejoicing over the dawn of a new era in both the realms of religion and literature. Their bright and shining light, the leader of the young and venerable hosts, is none other than the Rev. W. H. H. Murray, probably one of the most popular young clergymen ever settled in Boston, as he is one of the most renowned in the country. It is a year or more ago since internal dissensions of a creedy nature influenced him to resign his pastorate of the Park Street Church, in this city. Immediately after his resignation a movement to establish a new Union church, with Mr. Murray at its head, was conceived and carried forward by his most ardent admirers and supporters in the church from which he had just severed his connection. The result of all this was the sudden raising of funds for the erection of the largest church edifice in the United states, and within twelve months the sacred edifice will adorn the now vacant lot on the corner of Columbus avenue and Berkley street.[5]

According to historian H. Crosby Englizian, "Murray had said the solution to Boston's moral condition would be the formation of a metropolitan church where thousands could hear the saving gospel. Ambitiously, he felt a man large enough to hold an audience of three or four thousand each Sunday for ten years would make his opinions 'the opinions of thousands, and his faith, the faith of the rising generation.'"[6] Indeed, Murray had big plans. His new church was to "feature a one-thousand voice choir, a quartet, three services each Sunday and annual sitting rentals of ten dollars."[7]

Murray's published sermons for this period often reflected his apparent frustrations with orthodoxy and the denominational outlook of traditional Boston churches. For instance, he told his congregations that "[i]t is a very mockery of the beautiful and primal law of God touching the communication and common fellowship of goodness, that men will flock together, and form cliques and circles, shutting themselves up with sectarian and denominational lines, and strive to be dissimilar."[8] Murray was determined that his new church would be independent and blind to the restraints of denomination.

The *Boston Daily Globe* provides a glimpse into Murray's proceedings at the music hall and his desire to separate himself from the sectarian divisions of Boston:

Rev. W. H. H. Murray preached before the New England Church in Music Hall yesterday morning the subject, "The Church that Boston Needs," taking for his text Revelations, iii.,8: "Behold I have set before thee an open door." This sermon was the first of two upon the same subject and the hall was well filled. In beginning, the speaker said that he had been born and educated where denominational prejudices were almost unknown. The religious influence to which he had been accustomed were entirely orthodox, and he had had very little idea of the sectarian bitterness which exists in Boston. He had come here, therefore, well prepared to observe the religious feeling disinterestedly. His idea of a Universalist was that of a man who had a more hopeful belief concerning the salvation of men than the Orthodox had, and of a Unitarian that of a man who believed in God and himself and as much more as his mind was capable of. Said he: I found that your differences spring from egotism and ignorance of each other, and that with a finer modesty regarding your own opinions would come a more Christian-like regard for the opinions of others. I have done what I could to break prejudice down, and have striven for a union of all Christian souls on a natural, untheological, scriptural basis. The speaker continued by reviewing hastily the system of parish churches, which was inaugurated with the establishment of the colonies and showed wherein that system is now totally inadequate to the work which is before it. Your church system has not changed in forty years. Good men have tried to modify it without success. You might as well try to make the Town Government do the work of a city. There is too much tyranny in the parish church, and the sooner people device a metropolitan church system, the better. . . . The People are all the right. The fault is with the system which must be made to accommodate itself to the people, however fickle they may be. The speaker then proceeded to explain his plan for a church that would not be parish, nor a denomination church. A creed it will have, but it will be inclusive and not exclusive.[9]

Englizian sheds further light on Murray's Music Hall Independent Congregational Church: "Weekly services were held, with a Sunday school and a Monday evening devotional meeting. The music included congregational singing and a two-hundred voice choir under the direction of Professor Eben Tourjée. . . . In addition to the excellent musical and lecture program, church interest was maintained with the use of Murray's literary gifts. Special entertainments and sociables were frequently given, with Murray giving readings and recitations from his Adirondack tales."[10]

The inclusion of Dr. Eben Tourjée in the proceedings at Boston Music Hall is especially interesting to note. Tourjée was a Methodist, not a Congregationalist, and had founded the New England Conservatory of Music in 1867.[11] He was a regular attendee of the Tremont Street Methodist Episcopal Church and became a prominent leader within Boston's evangelical movement.[12] Influenced by the passionate sermons of Reverend W. R. Clark of the Tremont Street church, Tourjée became a prominent leader of the mission movement in Boston's North End. Murray, in turn, publicly praised the work of the North End Mission in 1875, stating that "the strength of the North End Mission lies with its personnel. In that field, good people have put themselves in contact with bad people, and Satan is being thwarted."[13] In addition, in 1869 Tourjée helped establish an industrial school in Boston's North End for the purpose of teaching women and children to sew, and, thus, a means to survive.[14] Like Murray, Tourjée was focused on the growing number of urban poor in Boston.

In 1872, Dr. Tourjée helped establish a music conservatory at Boston University and simultaneously served as dean of that school as well as his own New England Conservatory.[15] This is surely a strong indication of the widespread recognition and respect for the man's talent and ability.

By 1875, Tourjée was involved in the labor reform movement advocating for the women and children sewers who had been trained in the North End school.[16] Interestingly, this political involvement may have had a similar effect on Tourjée's wealthy supporters as Murray's activities had found at Park Street. Benjamin L. Harley writes:

Tourjée's political involvement on behalf of workers may have rubbed some of his more wealthy supporters the wrong way. His nephew remarked that "had he gone to Bombay or Hong

Kong, he would have been proclaimed a martyr for his noble gesture." Yet, it seemed to many both strange and remarkable for a man of his position to devote himself to the rescue of lost souls in his own city. Prior to this, most of Boston's so-called respectable class knew little about the notorious North End conditions. But . . . Dr. Tourjée shocked many out of their Puritanical smugness with his true, hard-hitting account of things.[17]

Thus, Murray's Music Hall Church included a choir leader who was not only a famed music school founder, but also actively involved in progressive movements in Boston. Tourjée would go on to lead the music of Boston's evangelical Moody Revival in 1877 and the thousand voice tabernacle choir included in that affair.[18]

When Dr. Tourjée resigned from his presidency at the North End Mission in 1876, he was, interestingly enough, replaced by Ezra Farnsworth, a well-to-do elder at Park Street Church. It seems the work of men such as Tourjée and Murray had begun to impact even the previously conservative and reticent Park Street Church members.

The Music Hall Independent Congregational Church capitalized on the fame Murray obtained at Park Street Church, and for a time it succeeded. Ruby Murray Orcutt described her father's time at the Boston Music Hall:

In '75, however, most of his former congregation having remained loyal to him, he was persuaded by its representatives to open an Independent Church. This he decided to do and for three years he addressed packed audiences at Music Hall. The place was filled to overflowing, camp chairs placed in the aisles and entrances, and it is recorded that even the steps and adjacent sidewalks were crowded.[19]

The Music Hall pastor was certainly paid well. Murray allowed himself an annual salary of $20,000,[20] an unheard of sum for a pastor in those days. Murray Orcutt continues:

At this period, my father was doubtless at the height of his career. He was in his middle thirties, possessed of tireless energy, enthusiasm, a burning desire to preach the truth as he saw it, a longing also for time to continue his creative work, with no taste whatever for the routine part of clerical life such as parish calls and social activities in general, with tremendous physical energy which necessitated the outlet afforded by his stock farm, his trips into the wilderness, his hunting and fishing, with the strong-headedness that was his from first to last, with exceeding personal charm which made him much sought after and exposed him to many temptations, not all of which he was able to resist.[21]

Murray Orcutt did not elaborate further on these "temptations" but it is safe to assume that they included both business and personal ambitions, which we will come to later.

~

During this period of success, Murray was also editing and publishing a periodical he founded named *The Golden Rule*.[22] This magazine combined Murray's sermons, other religious articles, and articles on the outdoors, including many concerning Murray's beloved outdoors. W. H. Merrill Jr., an associate editor of the *Boston Herald*, shared editorial duties with Murray and contributed content.

The Golden Rule wavered during these years between weekly and monthly magazine. By 1879, though, the publication was clearly a monthly one. Subscription to the magazine cost $2.50 annually; single copies were $0.25 each.[23] Its populist credo, printed on the inside cover of each edition, was stated plainly:

> It will be, as its plan and contents indicate, a Magazine for the people, and not for a selected literary, artistic or scientific class: a Magazine for the household, and all its members, and for home-making and home-loving readers everywhere.[24]

Each edition of *The Golden Rule* contained an Adirondack tale and sermon from Murray; other short stories; biographical sketches; articles on the household, including recipes and health tips; music; poetry; articles on rural matters; fashion; literature; and art. The magazine was designed to have a bit of something for everyone.

Through his own content and editorial role, Murray was able to use *The Golden Rule* to further his increasingly progressive advocacies. His printed sermons included those concerning Christian unity ("the reason so many doctrines plainly scriptural are being dropped as non-essential by people is found just here at this point. They are not associated with Christ"),[25] human equality ("the introduction of aristocratic churches among a democratic people, is such a folly and a wickedness as to find no palliation in the state of society and the temper of the times"),[26] Christian growth ("You cannot fence in a few utterances and say, within this enclosure can be found the truth"),[27] and seeing God ("Nature is full of God. She is divine through all her frame. All suspect it, many know it, but only a few apprehend it clearly and sensitively").[28]

Editorials included within the editions of *The Golden Rule* were similarly used by Murray. The editorial pieces discussed the plight of young urban men, supported the Women's Educational and Industrial Union of Boston, with suggestions regarding how to help the poor, patriotism, and proper home life. Contributors to the magazine provided support for Murray's causes, and included articles encouraging temperance and advocacy of the natural world.

～

Murray's move to Boston Music Hall and his ambitious plans to establish a large metropolitan church in Boston fit well within the evangelism that was enveloping Boston during this period. Murray's career had its beginnings in old-school theology, but his beliefs had clearly evolved over time and were much more progressive and liberal in nature by the mid-1870s. While Murray was not an evangelist in the strict sense of the word, it is important to examine evangelism in late-nineteenth-century Boston in order to better understand the world within which Murray was evolving and attempting to prosper in his role as minister.

Evangelist movements became increasingly popular in the United States during the nineteenth century, and the movement was quite diverse. Preachers to the urban masses, as well as their benefactors, came from diverse denominational backgrounds including Baptist, Methodist, and even the Salvation Army.[29] In many ways, Boston was at the center of evangelical and liberal Protestantism in America at the time. As Hartley writes: "The thick network of Protestant theological seminaries such as

Harvard (Unitarianism) Andover (Congregationalist) Newton (Baptist), Episcopal Theological School and Boston University School of Theology (Methodist Episcopal) all within a convenient commute from downtown Boston underscored the position of Boston as the intellectual center of American Protestantism."[30]

Though diverse in approach, the evangelical movements during Murray's time in Boston largely focused on both the sanctification of the whole individual and wide-reaching social reform movements. Boston's evangelical groups founded numerous city missions to address the needs of newly arrived immigrants and the urban poor. They founded orphanages and led labor reform, temperance, and women's rights movements in the city, addressing many of the same issues that Murray had begun to emphasize.

In the middle of Murray's career at the Boston Music Hall Church a huge evangelical revival came to the city of Boston. Dwight L. Moody selected Boston as the final stop of his two-year evangelistic tour.[31] The evangelism that Moody brought to Boston was part of the "holiness movement" begun prior to the Civil War. At the heart of the holiness movement was emphasis on the entire sanctification of the individual. This meant involvement in both individual salvation and social reform.[32]

In some sense, Moody's travel to Boston for his final revival stop was a homecoming. Born to a Western Massachusetts farm family, Moody had been converted from Unitarianism to a "heartfelt Christianity" when in a shoe store in downtown Boston in 1855.[33] This "heartfelt Christianity" was likely closer to Murray's "old-school theology" and the Protestantism found at Park Street Church than to the more liberal theology that Murray was then presiding over at Boston Music Hall.

Though Moody's education had not continued past the fourth grade, he developed a sharp, businesslike approach to his revivalism. Prior to bringing his revival to any city, Moody would insist that participating churches—most of which saw Moody's revival as a remedy against liberal theology—achieve some sort of unity of purpose with respect to the upcoming revival. Moody also actively engaged the local press to promote his revival work. The preparations in Boston followed this course, with at least seventy-eight churches in the city pledging support for the revival, including, Park Street Church. The city's newspapers provided Moody with the required pre-event promotion and printed daily stories about the revival during its run in Boston.[34]

The evangelist insisted that a new tabernacle be built in each city along his tour, and Boston was no exception. The Moody tabernacle in

Boston was constructed on Tremont Street, covered a full acre of ground, and was said to have capacity for seven thousand people.[35] Much like Murray's plan for the Boston Music Hall, the Moody Tabernacle included a thousand voice choir led, of course, by Dr. Eban Tourjée.[36] Unlike Murray, Moody actually achieved this boast.

The Moody revival in Boston lasted for three months and had a great impact on life in Boston during this time. As Hartley tells us:

> The echoes of Eben Tourjee's thousand-voice tabernacle choir and Moody's powerful preaching were felt throughout New England in the weeks and months following the Boston campaign's conclusion on April 30, 1877. . . . More than a million people were said to have walked through the tabernacle doors to hear the great evangelist and his coworkers. . . . Organizers estimated that as many as six thousand persons were converted at Moody's meetings.[37]

Moody's Revival in Boston took place daily and usually included several events each day. Many speakers, in addition to Moody himself, took the pulpit at the great Tabernacle Hall. Murray's friend Joseph Cook, the "Boston Monday Lecturer," was one such dignitary to share Moody's pulpit.[38]

The promised impact of Moody's Revival at each of its stops was the conversion of spirited Christians and, thus, increased church enrollment. While the revival led to increased church membership for some denominations in Boston, it was not true for the Congregationalist and Presbyterian churches within the city. It is unknown how the Moody revival and its aftermath impacted Murray's independent church at Music Hall, though Murray encouraged the Tabernacle to be kept and used "for the great urban providence of God to bloom and flower in."[39] It is certain, however, that during its three-month stop in Boston, the Moody Revival took center stage and necessarily cast the Murray church in deep shadow. Murray's warm words regarding Moody's Tabernacle stand in opposition to other statements attributed to him. In a short article titled "Popular Murrayism vs. Unpopular Spiritualism," the *Spiritual Scientist* wrote:

> We find that the Rev. W. H. H. Murray, in his Friday evening talk of March 9, alluded to Revivals, and advised the mothers to keep their boys in bed rather than send them to Mr. Moody's inquiry meeting; for says he: "It is a hot-bed of Spiritualism,

and the boys who attend these meetings will, I suspect, be the worst boys in the city ten years from now, unless God intervenes to save them. They are being fed with such food that they will dislike the taste of it in ten years."[40]

The magazine went on to state its position that despite Murray's protests and warnings, his belief system was liberal and nothing more than "diluted spiritualism."[41] Claiming that more than half of his congregation were spiritualist in belief if not name, the magazine explained that while at Park Street "he could easily see that 'Hell-fire, Devil, and brimstone' ideas pleased the remnants of old fogies of past generations, but the sons and daughters, the young men and women, preferred something more compatible with their common sense."[42]

~

As we have seen, it was remarked by some that W. H. H. Murray was in the same class as Henry Ward Beecher when it came to preaching. The two ministers were friendly and even occasionally switched congregations, with Beecher preaching at Park Street while Murray preached at Beecher's church in Plymouth, Massachusetts.[43] In this light, it might be said that Murray managed to surpass Beecher when it came to scandal. Beecher suffered much notoriety when his alleged affair with Elizabeth Tilton, wife of his friend Theodore Tilton, becoming the unwanted subject of a legal trial and national media attention.[44] But it appears that Beecher's transgressions were more limited then Murray's (at least to the extent such transgressions were made public). Here, perhaps, we begin to see some of the "temptations" that Ruby Murray Orcutt had alluded to.

The first public intimations of Murray's alleged transgressions regard his private secretary, Lilla Mabel Hodgkins. Hodgkins was born in Dexter, Maine, in 1856.[45] In 1879, she was described as a pretty, stylish, entertaining girl approximately twenty-two years old.[46] Murray was thirty-nine years old at that time.

Hodgkins's employment as Murray's private secretary corresponds with the time when his marriage with Isadora was evidently waning. The various newspaper accounts of Hodgkins involve her spending days in the wilderness alone with her employer and vehemently vouching for his veracity on several occasions. The newspapers of the day had an opportunity to catch up with Hodgkins in August 1869, when she was en route from Plattsburgh, New York, to New York City. At that time, Hodgkins denied that she and Murray had eloped. Murray was, according to her, headed to New York to meet with his attorney and friend Orville Platt. The man was exhausted and had sought recreation.[47]

Hodgkins explained her relationship with Murray to reporters at the *New York Sun:* "My family and Mr. Murray's have been friends for many years and Mrs. Murray is a very dear friend of mine. I took a notion to write for Mr. Murray and do odd things that nobody else would do, and thus I became his amanuensis several years ago."[48] Nonetheless, rumors of an untoward relationship between the Reverend Murray and Miss Hodgkins were not abated.

≁

When he was not preaching, writing, camping, or horsing around, Murray spent much of his time attempting to gain financial wealth. The problem was that W. H. H. Murray was a lousy businessman. One contemporary declared that "Murray was about the poorest business man I ever saw, while he thought he was the best—a false bottom to stand on in dollars and cents!"[49] This sentiment was echoed by Murray's most intimate friend H. J. Griswold, who proclaimed that the man "was certainly a great preacher and writer, but he lacked in business and executive ability and the worst of it was that he never fully realized this to the day of his death."[50] The historical record supports such observations.

As we have seen, *The Golden Rule* began as a weekly publication, and later morphed into a monthly paper when subscriptions would not support more frequent editions. The *Kingston Daily Freeman* seemed to attribute the failure of *The Golden Rule* to Murray's overambition and the claim that the minister "had undertaken to serve too many masters."[51] His ambitions for the magazine had proven misplaced, and the publication was sold by Murray to a company of Boston men who, according to newspaper accounts, planned to return *The Golden Rule* to a weekly paper. The Boston men who purchased *The Golden Rule* were Harrison A. Shorey (a former pastor at the Pilgrim Church in Dorchester, Massachusetts) and Charles W. Baldwin. The announcement of the magazine's sale was included in the June 1879 edition and readers were assured of Murray's continued involvement with and contribution to *The Golden Rule*.[52]

One of the distractions, and a possible "temptation" that Murray's daughter Ruby did not identify by name when speaking of her father's experiences in the 1870s, was the Boston Buckboard Company. The company was the manifestation of Murray's ambition to manufacture fine carriages and complimented his equine passions. To that end, Murray purchased a patent for a unique buckboard wagon, which he subsequently dubbed the "Murray Wagon," and the Boston Buckboard Company was incorporated in the state of Connecticut in 1879.[53]

Murray told the typically colorful story of the company's origins during an interview in San Francisco in 1879:

> At present I have about fifty head of horses, including colts, on the Guilford Farm, all of the Morgan strain. I consider it the most illustrious of the horse family. I know they are not fashionable now-a-days, but they are a race of kings. . . . My stallion Morgan Abdallah is as near a perfect horse as I want to see. Then there is my old favorite. Live Oak, now 18 years of age. He knew more than some men, and is used by me for general farm work. He has got some magnificent offspring. About two years ago I became acquainted with an itinerant peddler of patent medicines who had constructed a wagon on the principle of the buckboard for the purpose of carrying his medicines and avoid the necessity of jolting of the glass bottles. It appeared to me that the buckboard was too long in the reach, which rendered it too elastic. At my suggestion he made it considerably shorter, and finally we found that it worked like a charm. I remarked to him, "Now, Mr. Philips, you have a fortune in this thing. Go to work and have it patented." He replied that he had not sufficient means. Finally, to make a long story short, I assisted him financially, and the "Boston Buckboard Company" was organized to manufacture the wagons. They soon became popular, and had a large sale in New England.[54]

The company was initially well capitalized with $100,000. Murray held approximately $40,000 worth of stock in the company, and served as its vice president for a time.[55] The Boston Buckboard Company listed offices at 155 and 163 East Street in New Haven, Connecticut, where its manufacturing facility was located, as well as sales offices on Beacon Street in Boston and in Chicago.[56]

The company's formation, along with a typically Murray anecdote, was reported in the *New York Evening Post*:

Murray has succeeded in forming a company for making the "buckboard" wagon. It will have its headquarters in New Haven, will have a capital stock of $250,000 and will employ one hundred men. To the same gentleman the following story told by the Boston *Transcript* probably refers:

Not long since a well-known Boston minister and editor famed, quite as much for his love of horses and out-door sports as for "mildness, peace and prayer," was trying one of his pet nags on the Brighton road, when a gentleman came along with his pet nag, evidently ready for a "brush." He got all he wanted; the minister disappeared in a cloud of dust. Next day the two chanced to meet in the street. "How are you?" said the horse-loving divine, heartily. "You have the advantage of me, sir," answered the other. "You can't have forgotten that little race we had yesterday," continued the minister. "No, of course not, but a 'brush' on the road is one thing and subsequent acquaintance quite another. You must excuse me; horse-trainers are not in my line, socially," and he bowed, as if to close the interview. "You'll at least take my card," said the clergyman, who had to pucker his mouth to keep from laughing. His lofty highness condescended to take the pasteboard, and—came down.[57]

A description of the Murray Wagon was included in a report on the 1879 New England Fair, where it was displayed: "The Murray buckboard wagon was also on exhibition, and was greatly appreciated. Its springs are simple and peculiar, longitudinal and lateral, and its free and easy motion will likely make it popular."[58]

However, the Murray Wagon failed to meet expectations, and Murray's interest in the Boston Buckboard Company went the way of his other assets when its bottom eventually fell out. The company went on without Murray, and in 1885, it was reorganized as The Boston Buckboard and

Carriage Co. and devoted itself to the manufacture of light and medium carriages for the general trade.[59] The Murray Wagon was no more.

~

The mountains also continued to call Murray during the period of his independent ministry. Murray made his annual treks into the wilderness with his wife and friends and continued to write of the wilderness.[60] A powerful passion, the Adirondacks never lost their allure for Murray, despite the many twists and turns of his professional and personal life.

The business of the Murray Stock Farm continued through the mid- to late 1870s as well. There he was able to indulge his passion for fast horses—a passion that had earned him the moniker "William Henry Horse Murray." An inventory of Murray's assets during this period shows him as the owner of three houses, nine barns, a dozen dogs, and sixty horses.[61]

Then, on November 1, 1878, Murray had a serious accident while duck hunting with friends on the Long Island Sound. According to published reports, Murray's gun exploded in his hands when he pulled its trigger.[62] After walking nearly a mile to the nearest house, he was transported home and attended to. The result of the grisly incident was the loss of three fingers on Murray's right hand.

~

By 1879, Murray's life was at the peak of yet another mountain between deep valleys, and his course began to edge downward. After enjoying nearly five years of popularity outside of Park Street Church, the appeal—and correspondingly the attendance—of the independent church at the Boston Music Hall was waning. Murray closed the Music Hall Independent Congregational Church in 1879, and his other ventures quickly failed.

By late 1879 all of Murray's investments and business efforts had gone bust. Through poor business acumen and neglect, Murray had over-extended himself. His creditors began to circle; promissory notes were called, and property was attached. The Murray Stock Farm was an easy target for Murray's creditors, and it, along with the Murray Homestead, was soon lost:

A mortgage of $10,000 held by a Boston Man on the farm of Rev. W. H. H. Murray at Guilford, Conn., has just been foreclosed.

Mr. Murray having taken no steps to stay the execution. The stock once on the place is scattered throughout the country, and the famous "Murray Farm" exists only in memory.[63]

The man who had been at the top of the world a short time earlier fell hard. Having been the darling of the public eye for many years, Murray's financial failures were not allowed to go unnoticed. Newspaper headlines were full of juicy tales of Murray's troubles in 1879. *The New York World* published an article titled "Adirondack Murray's Affairs," summarizing the man's financial collapse.[64] *The Lowell Daily Courier* was pleased to give its reader an update on "Rev. W. H. H. Murray's Embarrassments."[65] The August 5, 1879, edition of that paper reported that Murray had been in Burlington, Vermont, in late July. He then crossed Lake Champlain on his yacht to Plattsburg, New York. At Plattsburg, Murray's yacht was attached for debt and Murray reportedly fled to Chicago. "Involuntary proceedings were soon begun against Rev. W. H. H. Murray."[66]

The following article, titled "What Ruineth the Minister," was published by *The New York Express*:

Too much horse and buckboard have laid him, financially, on his back. Some years ago when he wrote that remarkable tissue of fictions about the Adirondacks, that created a brood of pot hunters and did very much to ruin the great northern woods for all purposes of sport, he was a great man in his way. Since then, however, he has taken to running newspapers, fighting with his congregation, driving fast horses, and to cap the climax, organizing a "Boston Buckboard Company." For the manufacture of the Murray wagon. The result of all of which is that Rev. Murray's property at Guildford. Conn has been attached to pay his debts and Rev. Murray himself is *non est inventus*. IT is the old adage of the shoemaker sticking to his last over again. As a sensational preacher and story-writer, although his methods were not always commendable, Rev. Murray was a success, but fast horses and buckboard wagons are not precisely in the ministerial line, and Rev. Murray has been obliged to succumb to them.[67]

In response to the notoriety he was quickly earning through both rumor and true accounts of his conduct, Murray published a formal rebuttal to his detractors in the Boston newspapers. The following appeared in *The Boston Weekly Globe* on September 9, 1879:

A PLUMP DENIAL

Strong Statements by the Rev. W. H. H. Murray.

The Indignant Protest of an Injured Man.

He Gives the Lie Direct to Persistent Defamers.

Space is cheerfully accorded to the Rev. W. H. H. Murray for the following statement from him. It will be read with intense interest by every friend of the reverend gentleman:

To the Press of Boston:

Gentlemen,—It is the first time, I believe, that I have ever intruded upon the press with a personal statement. The fact that my affairs have of late been made the subject of public gossip and press comment is my apology for doing so at the present time. Your courtesy will be extended to me the more readily, perhaps, both because it is the first time in my life I have ever asked it and because, I can assure you, it will be the last. I can cover the few necessary points briefly. It has been said I went away clandestinely. It is false. I went on business, and my going was known to many. I had property to sell. I went to sell it. I had money to collect, and I went to try to collect it, I had losses to adjust, and I went to arrange them. I went openly to my destination. At San Francisco I roomed at a prominent hotel under my own name. I called on many business men. I was the guest of prominent citizens. I visited ranches, factories, mines; I attended churches and public meetings—in short, I worked to do what I went to do, and as any business man would act, I acted. Nor is there any doubt I should have accomplished all had not the unwise and unjust action of a few of my creditors in the east, and the slanderous lies of those, who, lacking virtue themselves, credit all others with a share of their looseness, interrupted me in my plans and labors with their miserable outbreak.

Touching My Financial Status

I have this to say: My current indebtedness was small, my time notes few. I had anticipated no stringency. But a failure to receive money from my business that I had relied on, and then a farther failure to effect a temporary loan I had counted on if needed, made it unexpectedly necessary for me to ask a favor of several of mv creditors. I had no doubt, when I left for the west, it would be granted, By all rules of courtesy and justice in business I should have been, for my property was large and growing in value constantly. But the parties saw fit to act otherwise, and attached $30,000 worth of property to pay less than $5000 of debt, and hurried to a forced sale. My property is thus essentially out of my hands and beyond my control. My creditors have assumed the responsibility. Very well. They may go ahead. They are welcome to all I have earned and laid up by years of toil. The estate is valuable enough if fairly administered to pay all claims against it, and leave a large surplus. If it does not, then, when the matter is settled I will go to work, if I have health, and pay every man what remains his due. But I will not raise my finger to help in such

Wicked Doing as Has Been Done Against Me.

They may rob and murder me, but I won't officiate at my own funeral. I won't assist them to make injustice respectable. A word about my public life: I retire from it. I utterly decline to remain in a service in which my noblest motives are traduced, my views grossly misinterpreted, and my best benevolence made the cause and ground of slanderous attacks. A life in which I can have no quiet, no peace, no friends; in which I can show no courtesies and do lip charities, unless at the risk of being vilely lied about and slandered, is one I refuse longer to live. The world, I have no doubt can get along well enough without me, and I am quite as certain I can get along well enough without the world. But this thing I say—and I take

All Who Know Aught of My Life

for the last fifteen years to witness the truth of it, that no good cause ever came to me for advocacy and did not get it; no poor person ever came to my study or office in want of food or clothes and was not, according to my means, assisted: and no vile man or intriguing woman ever entered my presence and did not depart kating and threatening me with such evil as they can work.

And now, leaving my property wholly to my creditors, and with my health seriously threatened, I turn from a manner of life I have ever disliked to a place and a mode of life I have ever loved. Henceforth I shall certainly escape the envy, and, I trust, the malice, of men. It would seem that I have done enough of good to have been treated differently, but it may be I am mistaken or what has been would not have come.

But it doesn't matter.

Very truly, W. H. H. Murray.[68]

Murray was also asked about his financial affairs during an interview in San Francisco:

"Mr. Murray," asked the reporter, "do you consider your business affairs to be as bad as represented by the Eastern papers!"

"When I left home I thought everything was in a snug condition, but I am sorry to say that some weeks ago a personal friend of mine who held my note, which was overdue, for $1,200, sued it and issued an attachment on some of my Guilford property. As soon as this was known, my creditors began to push things, and the usual result followed. My entire indebtedness will not exceed $19,000, and if my property was sold under the hammer tomorrow, it would be ample to pay them off and leave me a handsome surplus. There, I guess I, have told you everything."[69]

Murray's financial collapse at the end of the 1870s was certainly due to his ineptness when it came to business and investments, as well as the neglect that necessarily came to one well known as a "miscellaneous man." However, his collapse should not be viewed in a vacuum. The general economy of the United States throughout the 1870s was shaky at best.

What became known as the Long Depression and sometimes, before 1930, the "Great Depression," began with the Panic of 1873. Historians attribute many causes to the panic, including post–Civil War inflation, speculative investments, a large trade deficit, impacts from the Franco-Prussian War, and property losses in the urban fires of Chicago and Boston. All of these occurrences, and likely more, placed a massive strain on bank reserves, which plummeted in New York City during September and October 1873 from $50 million to $17 million.

The Panic of 1873 set off a worldwide economic depression that lasted for most of the 1870s.[70] During this time, building construction came to a halt; employee wages were cut; property values decreased, often dramatically; and corporate profits were significantly diminished, if not wiped out entirely.

The United States and Great Britain were hit particularly hard by this depression. The economic contraction caused by the Panic of 1873 lasted for sixty-five months, measured from October 1873 to March 1879. In the United States, some eighteen thousand businesses and ten state governments went bankrupt during this period, and unemployment reached anywhere from 8.25 to 14 percent.[71]

The financial turmoil sparked by the Panic of 1873 continued throughout the decade for Europe and the United States. There were work stoppages and layoffs throughout America, as well as many corporate losses. The National Bureau of Economic Research dates the contraction following the panic as lasting from October 1873 to March 1879.[72] At sixty-five months, it is the longest-lasting contraction identified by the bureau, eclipsing the forty-three months of contraction in the 1930s.[73]

Murray hit his financial height and bottom during a period of substantial economic strife in the United States. To his credit, he was able to demand high pay and accumulate much wealth during a period when the average American suffered greatly under a global economic depression. Had he been a sharper businessman and generally more attentive to his affairs, Murray might have been able to carry his success forward. This was not to be, however, his lot in life. In 1879, the man stood in financial ruin. He fled New England and his creditors, leaving behind a bewildered wife and many confused and shocked followers.

It was not in Murray's nature to disappear forever, and the sensation that seemed to follow the former preacher wherever he went guaranteed that the late-nineteenth-century newspapers would not let him vanish from the public eye, even if he had so desired. Less than ten years after his hasty and controversial departure, Murray gave two back-to-back lectures in his old haunt, the Boston Music Hall. The title and topic of the second lecture was "How to Become a Millionaire."[74]

$\sim$

Murray's woes during this period did not stop at financial ruin. His long run as celebrity preacher, author, lecturer, and horseman had apparently separated him too often from his wife. After nearly seventeen years of marriage, Bill and Isadora Murray formally separated on July 1, 1880.[75]

Happily, though, while Murray had busied himself with church, wilderness, and horses, Isadora, still without children to tend to, had not been idle. Instead, Mrs. Murray had developed a keen interest in medicine. The separation from her husband allowed her to formally pursue this growing passion, and she enrolled in the New York Medical College for Women.[76]

Isadora's pursuit of a degree in medicine during the latter part of the nineteenth century is a testament to her bold character. Graduating from the women's college on April 5, 1878, she went on to study homeopathic medicine in Dresden, Germany, and Vienna, Austria.[77] Dr. Isadora Murray became the first American woman licensed to practice surgery in Europe. In a letter to Murray, whom she called "Willie," written while she studied abroad, Isadora explained that "I have no ambition for reputation, never giving it a thought. It seems very small and belittling to one's nature to have such a selfish and ignoble aim; I only have a great desire to be able intelligently to diagnose, prescribe and if necessary operate for the benefit of my patient."[78]

When she returned to the United States, Isadora practiced medicine for many years in New Haven, Connecticut.[79] A contemporaneous newspaper account stated that her "success here in her chosen profession is proving great" and that she had "performed several dangerous operations in a safe manner."[80]

Isadora Murray never remarried. An 1884 article in the New York *Daily Tribune* described her parlor in her house in New Haven:

On the parlor wall hangs a large crayon portrait of Mr. Murray and oil paintings of the two horses in which she once took great delight, Abdallah and Star of the South.[81]

Isadora died at the age of eighty on November 9, 1925, in Springfield, Massachusetts, and was buried in Madison, Connecticut.[82]

~

When the Boston Music Hall church came to an end, along with Murray's other financial interests and, indeed, his marriage, Murray allegedly took Lilla Mabel Hodgkins with him as he retreated to Texas. The Essex County *Republican* later reported the following shocking news:

> V.A. Fenner, formerly of Sherman, Connecticut, writing from San Antonio, Texas, says that among the noted residents of the vicinity is the Rev. W. H. H. Murray, "Adirondack Murray" as he is called. When he fled from Boston his private secretary, a young lady, followed his fortunes and has since lived with him. Last year her father came for her, and after an effort to get her to return with him, which proved ineffectual, the poor old man, broken in spirit and almost penniless after his long search for her, blew out his brains at the very threshold of Murray's door.[83]

While it is not known whether it refers to Hodgkins and her father or is even true, the story implies that Hodgkins's father pursued the couple to Texas and ended his own life there upon his failure to redeem his daughter. Like that of Isadora Murray, the story of Hodgkins is intriguing beyond her involvement with Murray. In January 1882, Hodgkins married Reverend James S. McCoy in New York City and thereafter went by the name Mabel McCoy.[84] The couple then moved to Tombstone, Arizona. After several years in Arizona, the McCoys divorced and Mabel McCoy returned east to New York City.[85]

In 1892, after some time as a faith healer and one year at the Meadville Theological School in Pennsylvania, McCoy joined ten other women enrolling in Tufts Divinity School, which had recently become a coeducational institution.[86] In her first year at Tufts, McCoy joined a fraternity and assisted that organization in opening the first fraternity chapter house on the Tufts campus. McCoy did not return to Tufts after that first year but went on to become a Universalist minister at First Parish Church in Mansfield, Massachusetts. She is credited with being the second woman ordained in Massachusetts.[87]

W. H. H. Murray with Rifle.

Before and after going into the Adirondacks. From *Harper's New Monthly Magazine*, August, 1870.

Harper's Cartoon.

PARK STREET CHURCH, BOSTON.

Park Street Church.

Vol. IV.   JANUARY.   No. 1.

THE GOLDEN RULE

—AN— ILLUSTRATED FAMILY MAGAZINE.

EDITED AND PUBLISHED BY
W. H. H. MURRAY.
BOSTON, MASS.

W. H. H. MURRAY.

1879

CONTENTS

$2.50 A YEAR.   25 CENTS A COPY.

The Golden Rule.

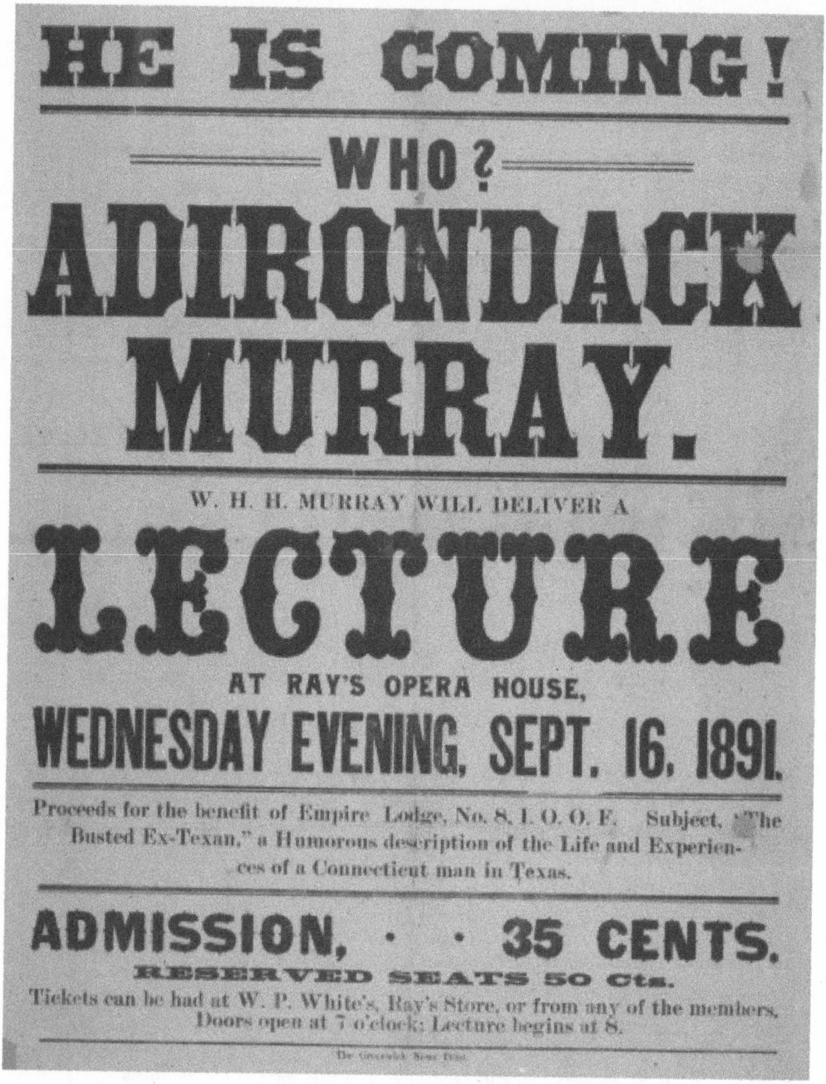

HE IS COMING!

WHO?

ADIRONDACK MURRAY.

W. H. H. MURRAY WILL DELIVER A

LECTURE

AT RAY'S OPERA HOUSE,

WEDNESDAY EVENING, SEPT. 16, 1891.

Proceeds for the benefit of Empire Lodge, No. 8, I. O. O. F. Subject, "The Busted Ex-Texan," a Humorous description of the Life and Experiences of a Connecticut man in Texas.

ADMISSION, · · 35 CENTS.

RESERVED SEATS 50 Cts.

Tickets can be had at W. P. White's, Ray's Store, or from any of the members. Doors open at 7 o'clock; Lecture begins at 8.

He is Coming Broadside.

ADIRONDACK MURRAY

OPERA HOUSE,

PALMER, MASS.,

Friday Evening, Nov. 5th, 1897

Mr. W. H. H. Murray will read that sweet story of

The Dear Old Trapper, John Norton, and How He Kept His Christmas.

Professional elocutionists, literary critics, and the people, are in full agreement touching the "sweetness and light" of this little tale of wood life and the woods, and the lovableness of him whom so many call

"Dear Old John Norton."

This story has been read FIVE HUNDRED AND THIRTY-FIVE TIMES IN NEW ENGLAND ALONE.

No bit of writing has ever been received by Lyceum audiences with greater favor.

If you have heard it I known you will hear it again. If you have not heard it come and hear from Mr. Murray's own lips this, his masterpiece.

TICKETS, 50 AND 35 CENTS.
ON SALE AT ALLEN'S DRUG STORE.
SECURE YOUR SEATS EARLY.

Mail orders to C. E. Fish and Telephone orders to the Palmer Journal office will receive prompt attention.

C. B. Fiske & Co., Printers, Palmer.

Adirondack Murray Broadside.

Buffalo Bill Group Photo.

Live Oak.

PART THREE

MISCELLANEOUS MAN

Chapter 12

Texas

I never wrote a line for a paper in Texas. I never speculated.

—W. H. H. Murray

Unlike Isadora Murray's, W. H. H. Murray's life was not so focused following the couple's separation in the summer of 1880. For the first time since his years at Yale, Murray, now forty years old, was without a wife. With the failure of his independent church, he also was a minister without a flock.

Finding himself somewhat cut loose, Murray decided to flee his pressing financial woes and wander. True to character, he described this period of his life in a more flattering and purposed manner:

At the close of these 15 years of service he retired from the ministry and the clerical profession and entered upon a course of study best cultivated in his opinion for authorship and the platform, broadly interested—he went abroad and made a thorough examination of English commercial methods, her land system, and tendency of her social and political forces. He remained a close observer of the great battle between Gladstone and D'Israeli which ended with triumph of the former and then returned to his own country and entered upon a study of the resources and characteristics of this continent. This investigation he devoted six years and when he has returned from his present extensive tour he will have personally visited with the exception of Alaska every representative section of the Continent between Hudson's Bay and the Gulf of Mexico and between Newfoundland and Vancouver.[1]

Put a bit more bluntly, during the early years of the 1880s, the famous preacher, sportsman, and horseman became largely itinerant. Finding that his best source of ready income came from his lectures on the wilderness and outdoor life, Murray began to tour the lecture circuits of the United States and Europe; he even traveled to South Africa during this period.[2] Though less popular than a decade before, the lectures provided enough income to sustain Murray's travel and living arrangements.

Murray's private secretary, Lilla Mabel Hodgkins, was not the only female who enjoyed his company during this period of his life. A review of the surviving written record, comprised predominately of personal correspondence, reveals the existence of several women who became entangled with Murray during the period between his separation from Isadora and his second marriage. These records indicate that at least one of these women became a trusted, intimate confidante of Murray and was even entrusted with the management of his publications.

This trusted confidante, who began to appear in public with Murray during this period, was Fannie Bursley. In an account published in 1879 by *The Oswego Palladium*, Bursley is described as a tall, handsome, stylishly dressed blonde.[3] It is unknown how Bursley met Murray, but the surviving record makes it clear that the two were close and that Bursley was young enough to be passed off as the reverend's daughter.

Bursley lived with the former minister in the early 1880s. They traveled together extensively, making appearances as far away as San Francisco.[4] There, Bursley was said to be traveling not only with Murray but also with a second young woman, Mary Gallagher, described by *The San Francisco Chronicle* as a brunette and quite dashing Irish beauty.[5] The *Chronicle* reported that Gallagher was the traveling companion of Bursley and that Bursley, in turn, traveled for her health under the fatherly care of Reverend Murray.

The Brooklyn Daily Eagle reported at this time that "Murray is in San Francisco in company with Captain and Miss Bursley and Miss Mary Gallagher. Mr. Murray and his female companions left the overland train at Sacramento and waited for an afternoon local train, in order to reach the city at a time when their arrival would be less likely to be noticed. They stopped at the Arlington Hotel and the women registered under the names of Miss May and Miss Henry. Mr. Murray did not register at all. . . . Mr. Murray has avoided meeting acquaintances since his arrival in the city, and his actions have been marked in mystery."[6]

During an interview in San Francisco, Murray was asked about his traveling companions:

> "Mr. Murray, excuse me," hesitatingly inquired the reporter, with an effort to agitate a blush, "but would you be so kind as to tell me who the young ladies were who traveled in your company across the continent?"
>
> "Ha! ha!! that's natural enough," ejaculated the divine, with a hearty laugh. "Well, one was Miss Bursley, daughter of an old friend of mine who now lives in San Francisco, and the other is Mary Gallagher, a girl who worked in my family for four years, and also worked for some relatives of Miss Bursley in New York. Miss Bursley heard through my wife that I was coming to California, and wrote to me in Chicago, requesting that I would allow her to travel under my protection. Mary had caught the California fever, having heard of the high wages girls were receiving here, and thought she would come too. When we arrived here I took the girls to the Arlington House, where the Captain met then, and I went to the Russ. After remaining there awhile I moved to the Arlington and took a room there. That's the affair in a nutshell."[7]

The San Francisco Chronicle followed the activities of the eastern threesome during their stay in the city, confirming that the trio stayed at the Arlington House. The two young women shared a room on a different floor from the one Murray occupied. The three made it publicly known that they were in San Francisco awaiting the arrival of a Captain Bursley and evidently spent the interim entertaining themselves around the city. Captain Bursley never appeared, and the Chronicle reported that the Arlington House asked the three travelers to leave as their presence was against the "policy of the house."[8] Bursley, Gallagher, and Murray then disappeared for a bit only to be found occupying a small cottage on the outskirts of San Francisco. Despite later claims by Murray that his trip to San Francesco was open and business related, The New York Evening Telegram reported that the man disguised himself by growing a full beard and dressing as a railroad man or a well-to-do trader.[9]

~

Following these California escapades and a brief return east, Murray found himself in Texas.[10] It is said that during this time he tried his hand at ranching but that this was a failure. However, in a *New York Times* article dated April 6, 1883, Murray is quoted as denying with laughter that he ever had a ranch.

The state of Texas in the 1880s was far removed from the Gilded Age that had swept over in the eastern part of the United States. It remained a vast and largely unsettled land, with a few, widely spaced ostentatious displays of wealth and industrialization.[11]

Texas was growing, though. Through a steady stream of migration from the South, the population of Texas grew from 1.5 million to 2.2 million people in the decade between 1880 and 1890.[12] Most of the population was rural, with farming and ranching as the most popular livelihoods. Other major industries included lumber and flour milling. San Antonio, where Murray settled, was a relatively prosperous area after the Civil War. The city became a modernizing cattle distribution hub, as well as mercantile and military center of the region. The population of Murray's San Antonio numbered just above twenty thousand people.[13]

Murray may not have been a failed rancher, but his love of horses was certainly not abated during his time in Texas. An 1883 report by Murray championed the cross-breeding of the mustangs that Murray discovered in the West with thoroughbreds. Murray wrote that "Texas was just the place for horse breeding, and that the tough little mustangs are the right stock to take hold of for improvement."[14] The *Herald* continued: "Mr. Murray advises a cross from a thoroughbred stallion, believing that it would increase the size without losing toughness, and produce the best saddle horse, as well as trotter."[15]

Murray did try his hand in the lumber business while in Texas. With three other partners, two of whom were back east in Boston, Murray founded the Texas Hardwood Lumber Company and located it about fifty miles outside of San Antonio.[16] In an April 6, 1883, news article, Murray reported:

> I have been in San Antonio two years and a half, and went into the lumber business six months after going there. I went there two months after my return to New York City from London

with the intention of undertaking the negotiation of certain Texas lands in London.[17]

The article was written after Murray arrived in New York City, having left San Antonio, and largely concerns itself with Murray's refutation of certain scandalous rumors involving his time in Texas. Murray and one of the partners in the Texas Hardwood Lumber Company had a falling out, resulting, Murray claimed, in the spreading of rumors of Murray's unscrupulousness.[18] These rumors included Murray's flight from Texas due to debt and his having kept company with the young woman who had been his amanuensis in Boston. Murray adamantly denied both accusations.

On April 7, 1883, an article appeared in *The San Francesco Examiner* recounting Murray's return to the East Coast.[19] The article reported that Murray had arrived in New York City from San Antonio alone and had immediately gone to the house of Edwin T. Copeland in Brooklyn, staying there until the next day, when he removed himself to the Astor House. Here, Murray responded to the claim that he left Texas indebted to creditors there in the amount of $12,000:

> I do not owe $500 in Texas, all told, nor did I promise to meet any creditors on the afternoon of the day I left. No creditors asked me to pay. The story about my female amanuensis is false. I have been absolutely alone for the two and half years I have been in Texas. I passed the last month at the house of my lawyer. I came on alone. No man holds my notes for $2500. I never had a ranch in Texas and never bred cattle. I never failed in newspaper editing there.[20]

When asked why he had gone to San Antonio, Murray responded: "I went there from Denton, England, two years and a half ago to look after some land belonging to Englishmen."[21] The reporter then asked him about the status of his stock farm and buckboard company. To this Murray stubbornly replied:

> Those matters have not been settled up. Under Massachusetts law no one can examine my books without my consent, and I am in no hurry. I shall take a good five years' rest, and then I will attend to those matters. I shall then have something to

say as to the slanders that are constantly circulated about me. It's a d . . . n shame, publishing such stories.[22]

Not long after Murray's return to the East Coast from Texas, he turned his sights north to Canada, specifically to Montreal.

Chapter 13

Montreal

Mr. Murray is said to live in a very quiet and unassuming place . . . apparently devoting his entire time to the café business and quiet literary work.

—"Murray's Café"

The 1880s found Montreal well situated within its own golden age. Inhabiting an island in the St. Lawrence River, only sixty miles north of the New York State border, the city of Montreal had long been an important hub for commerce and culture in North America. By the 1880s, the city's population had grown to approximately 150,000, making Montreal the largest city in British North America.[1] In fact, Montreal had become the undisputed hub of commerce in Canada. St. James Street was the Wall Street of Canada, and business interests such as the Canadian Pacific Railway established their headquarters within the city limits.[2]

Historically hosting a francophone culture like the rest of the Province of Quebec, during the 1880s Montreal took on a more English character.[3] The northern city was wealthy and vibrant, and largely anglophone, when Murray arrived there in 1883. One cannot doubt that it was this vibrancy, among other things, that attracted the retired minister to Montreal. Murray's stay in Montreal lasted a little more than two years. However, much like his time in Texas, little is known about his life there. What we do know involves a small café and oyster bar, the most famous Wild West show of all time, and a young woman from New Brunswick.

Murray delivered several lectures on his beloved Adirondacks and outdoor life in general during his stay in Quebec. However, these certainly were not frequent enough to sustain his living for over two years. Instead, the former minister tried his hand in the restaurant business. In 1884, Murray opened a small oyster restaurant on the island and named it The Snowshoe. The restaurant was located at 1691 Notre Dame Street.[4] According to one account, the restaurant was "a neat little box, and the waiters are pretty women. . . . As a special favor to friends or distinguished visitors he sometimes presides at the open coal fireplace cooking oysters in batter and butter or broiling a fish or a bird. His experience in camping out in the woods and his fondness for cooking make his culinary productions much sought after."[5] A report in *The New York World* claimed that Murray called his "respected sister" from Boston to Montreal to help him run little restaurant on Notre Dame Street.[6] A *Kansas City Times* article on the café mentioned Murray's married sister, but also a "Miss Fannie" who assisted Murray at the café.[7] Miss Fannie was "a tall, graceful lady with golden hair."[8] Murray's dedication to the virtues of the temperance cause was evident in Montreal, and The Snowshoe was known in the city as a temperance café.

In 1885 Murray's café closed. This may have been due to the wave of smallpox that struck the northern city that year. As one Boston newspaperman reported: "He has been compelled to close his eating house and is once more in the lecture field. . . . A very familiar figure in his eating house was a woman who presided at the case desk, and whom everyone knew as 'Murray's blonde.' Two weeks ago she showed signs of small pox and immediately left the Dominion."[9]

❧

In the summer of 1885, Buffalo Bill's Wild West show ventured north of the border into Canada for the first time. The famous traveling show came to Montreal in August of that year.[10] The dramatic show proved wildly popular in Montreal, selling out each of its six scheduled afternoon performances.[11]

The daily performances of the Wild West Show cost fifty cents to attend and were crowd-pleasers.[12] The site of the show was the Montreal Driving Park in Pointe St. Charles, just south of the city's busy port. Normally the venue for year-round trotting meets, the park was large enough to accommodate both the show and the large crowds it attracted.

With Bill Cody that summer came the famous Native American warriors Sitting Bull and Crow Eagle, along with live buffalo and mustangs.[13] The show allowed the citizens of Montreal a glimpse into the storied life of the American West, and the crowds ate it up. Some six thousand people were in attendance at the last performance of Buffalo Bill's Wild West show in August. The mayor of Montreal spoke at this last show, praising Cody and his troupe for bringing the show to Montreal and educating its citizens on the trials and triumphs of the American West. W. H. H. Murray also addressed Cody and the crowd on this occasion, praising the show and its depiction of western life. Murray's involvement with the Wild West Show in Montreal is commemorated by a photograph the author took with the show's central cast, including Cody, Sitting Bull, and Crow Eagle.[14] Annie Oakley performed in Montreal as well, but evidently did not attend the picture session with Murray.

Murray seems to have been impressed by Chief Sitting Bull, though it is unknown how much time the two men were in each other's company during the show's week in Montreal. Sitting Bull was only with the show for four months, so it was serendipitous that the two men met in Montreal.[15] Later, when the murder of Sitting Bull at the Standing Rock Indian Reservation in the Dakotas was reported in 1890,[16] Murray's progressive thinking again came to the forefront. He was enraged at the murder of the great chief. In a December 21, 1890, article on the subject in *The New York World*, Murray blamed the death on greedy Indian agents: "The lying, thieving Indian agents wanted silence touching past thefts and immunity to continue their thieving."[17] Murray lamented the loss of the great chief and prophesized that one day Sitting Bull would be revered. He continued:

> I read that they have buried his body like a dog's, without funeral rites, without tribal wail, with no solemn song or act. This is the deed of to-day. That is the best that this generation has to give to this noble historic character. . . . Very well. So let it stand for the present. But there is a generation coming that shall reverse this judgment of ours. Our children shall build monuments to those whom we stoned and the great aboriginals whom we killed will be counted by the future American as among the historic characters of the Continent.[18]

~

It is likely that, in looking back to his time in Montreal, Murray would name neither Buffalo Bill's Wild West Show nor his experience as a restaurateur on Notre Dame Street as the highlight of his stay. Rather, Murray's meeting of a young woman from New Brunswick would inhabit his most cherished memories in Montreal.

Frances Mary Rivers was born in the Canadian maritime province of New Brunswick on March 26, 1858. The Rivers family lived in Pokemouche, New Brunswick, and was fairly wealthy, its male members having established themselves as successful bankers and landowners. Both sides of Frances's family were primarily of English descent. Her father was Michael Bartley Rivers, and her paternal grandfather was Thomas Rivers. Thomas had immigrated to Canada from Waterford, Ireland, where the Rivers family had settled after leaving England some years earlier. Frances's mother was Esther Sewell. Esther was born on May 24, 1834, and lived a long life, passing away on November 13, 1918 (her husband Michael died on May 17, 1864). Like her husband, she was first-generation Canadian. Her father, Joseph Sewell, emigrated from Cumberland County in the northwest corner of England to Pokemouche in 1814, a year before Thomas Rivers.

As a young woman, Frances moved from her childhood home of Pokemouche to Montreal. Trained as a telegrapher, she found work with the Canadian Pacific Railway and was working there when she met W. H. H. Murray. Having courted and fallen in love with this younger woman from New Brunswick, Murray decided that he wanted Frances to become his wife. To facilitate this, he moved from Montreal and traveled south to Burlington, Vermont, on the shores of Lake Champlain, with plans to marry.

Chapter 14

Burlington

Naturally, the book, because of the fame it won, became, as years passed, my knowledge grew apace and my powers of expression ripened, a regret to me. It did not represent me as an author.

—W. H. H. Murray, *Mamelons and Ungava*

Public reports of Murray's relocation to Burlington, Vermont, began to circulate in November 1885.[1] Apparently, Murray left Montreal before his bride-to-be in order to get settled and prepare for their new life. As a Canadian citizen, Frances Rivers's entry into the United States was noted in 1886.[2] Crossing the border, she went on to Burlington where she and Murray planned to marry. The courtship of Rivers by Murray did not go unnoticed, and here his scandalous behavior with Hodgkins and Bursley, among others, raised its head.

Individuals had long observed and taken note of the former minister's unorthodoxy. In the late 1880s it seems that some observers even went so far as to seek to prevent more young ladies from falling under his spell. One such individual was Nathan Clarke of Boston. Clarke wrote at least two missives to Frances Rivers, pleading with her to flee the former minister. Clarke wrote:

I am a man past fifty, I have known Mr. Murray ever since he first came to Boston, I bear him no malice, but write to save one woman from the merciless unhappiness to which I have seen him bring <u>so many</u>. He is married and the divorce he claims is not settled. If it were he would not marry although he has always promised each young woman she should be his wife some day. . . . If you have not already given your virtue into the hands of this fascinating evil doer for God's sake <u>stop</u> where you are for <u>no matter what</u> presents he will make and promises so gilded by his oratorical ability no matter what turn now while you may on him or your life's happiness is cast from you.[3]

Not satisfied to admonish Rivers without furnishing examples of Murray's outrageous behavior, Clarke continued:

He has two young ladies at his home whom he tries to pass off as adopted daughters to the public. Let us hope they are this and no more, but I have known him sixteen years and am growing old and do not tell you this for ought but your good having seen other women sweet as you accursed by him.[4]

He closed this first letter with news of an impending trip to California and his intent to check in with Rivers upon his return to know her decision.

Apparently, Clarke could not wait for his return to Boston to check in with Rivers, as his second letter was sent from San Francisco on April 5, 1886.[5] Having not heard from Rivers, he wrote:

My dear Young Lady

After writing you as I did I bethought you would at once send to Mr. Sewall my note asking for an explanation. I warned you of his eloquent arguments for himself and know well he will say it is only some one trying injure him but this is not so. Men could injure him by such facts as I gave you but a young woman like you could not and hence you will see my object was only to protect you against the damnable results which have come under my eye and of which I hold letters left me by one in his unmistakable hand writing with all the promised lies of wifehood. No I shall never write you again but God grant you character and power to resist this <u>eloquent fascinator</u> of both old and young women and thus save yourself. Keep this to yourself and Heaven guard you. I had a daughter and love of her happiness makes me wish to shield all others. I wish you had replied to my letter but will feel I have done a duty and rest in peace.[6]

Thus it appears that Clarke attempted to save an innocent, young woman from the grasp of the eloquent fascinator W. H. H. Murray.[7]

~

Frances Rivers was not persuaded by Mr. Clarke's missives, however, and she pursued the marriage bond with Murray. On October 11, 1886, at 8 pm, Murray, then forty-six years old, and Frances Rivers were married. The ceremony was a civil one, performed by a Justice Foster, because Rivers was Catholic.[8]

The Burlington Free Press's announcement of Murray's marriage on October 11, 1886, to Frances Rivers,[9] contains an intriguing note concerning the attendance at the ceremony of Murray's daughter and her rumored engagement. The paper reported that Murray's daughter was said to be headed to England to live with her future husband. While the engagement would certainly be interesting news to Murray followers, that Murray had a daughter of legal age in 1886 would have surely shocked many, since he and his first wife Isadora had no offspring.

Despite bearing the same last name, the young woman referenced in the 1886 wedding announcement was not Murray's daughter, at least not in any traditional meaning of that word. The woman went by the name of F. Marguerita Murray. The paper's account of her engagement was true. At the time of its writing, the woman was engaged to be married to Harry George Gear of England, and she later moved to England with her new husband. But who was she to Murray?

F. Marguerita Murray was the new name of Fannie Bursley. Following her travels with Murray to the west, Bursley had adopted Murray's last name and the new persona of Marguerita. This change in name was likely at the urging of Murray in an attempt to keep up appearances. As we will see, Marguerita Murray was not only present at the wedding, but continued to play a role in the new couple's life for many years.

~

Bill and Frances Murray lived in Burlington, Vermont, for nearly five years after their marriage in 1886. By all accounts, the Murrays were personally happy during their years there. Frances gave birth to the couple's first child, Maud Marguerite Murray, on June 8, 1887, and a second daughter, Ruby Rivers Murray, quickly followed on November 19, 1888.

The Murrays had at least two residences in Burlington during this period. The couple first appear in the 1888–89 Burlington City Directory.[10] In that directory, the couple are listed as residing in a house at the northeast corner of North Bend (later known as North Avenue) and North Cove Road, just north of the city and not far from the mouth of the Winooski River. In the 1889–90 directory, the Murrays are listed as living at 244 North Avenue.[11] The couple was not alone in Burlington however, as Marguerita Murray continued to play a significant role in their lives.

Murray's relationship with the person he called Marguerita Murray was evidently one of love and great trust, for he placed in her care what were likely some of his most prized possessions—his written works. For a time, Marguerita held Murray's power of attorney and managed the publication of his works. A close examination of period copies of his books reveals that even the copyrights of many are in the name of F. Marguerita Murray.[12] Marguerita, often listed as F. M. Murray, was also the manager of Murray's Lecture Bureau, a literary syndicate formed to manage Murray's books, lectures, and readings, the letterhead of which contained the following message: "I beg to inform you that I have sole charge of my Father's interest and engagements whether connected with the Platform or the Press, and should be consulted by all parties desiring his Published Works, or his services as Lecturer or Reader."

In the 1889–90 Burlington City Directory, Fannie Marguerita Murray is listed as occupying a house at 252 North Avenue, just down the street from Bill and Frances.[13] When separated, Marguerita and Bill wrote many letters to each other, providing the only remaining direct evidence of their profound relationship. Marguerita's words reveal an intimate longing between them:

> I grieve very much that I did not insist upon remaining longer and spending a month with you at the farm. Regrets are useless. Fate is unkind and I feel she was most unkind the day we did not meet, it seems so wrong for us to have missed each other.
>
> How kind of you with so many correspondents to write me so often. I am coming home and a home, be it ever so

humble, is about all I want now to make the rest of my life content; I have drifted about for so long I am weary [*sic*], society is a farce, full of masked faces each covering an aching dissatisfied heart and a burdened soul.

Please make no mention of the contents of this letter at present, it makes a fitting separation for us both, before all that world of which we have been so much a part, gives you full release from all obligations.[14]

During his stay in Burlington, another Texas relationship also came to light in the most unpleasant of ways. Annie Ferguson, a young woman from Austin, Texas, became close to both Marguerita and Murray. In a letter to Murray, Marguerita began, "Love, such as mine has been for you and Annie, pure and unselfish, knows nor recognizes no such word as burden in the vocabulary of its services."[15] A harrowing letter dated March 18, 1887, from Mrs. A. M. Locke to Murray provides a bit more insight:

Dear Sir

There is a report in circulation here that my Annie died about five months ago. . . . Will you let me know if their report is <u>true</u> or <u>not</u>—I wrote to Miss Fannie on the subject over a month ago, but have received no answer yet. . . . Any and all information you will give me concerning my child will be most gratefully received. If you have reasons for keeping me from knowing her address or circumstances (i.e. her wishes of course. I know you have none of your own) tell me at least <u>she yet lives</u>, if not how when & where she died? And where buried? I can't bear this suspense much longer but think of her when awake and dream of her when asleep.[16]

It is not known whether Murray replied to Locke about the disposition of Ferguson. However, he did make a handwritten notation in the top margin of the first page of Locke's letter: "she was buried August 14, 1886, Burlington Vt."[17] In fact, Ferguson died on August 13, 1886, and was buried in a plot that Murray had purchased in the Lake View Cemetery[18] off North Avenue in Burlington. Her tombstone lists her name as Annie M. F. Murray and cites that she was the adopted daughter of W. H. H. Murray.[19]

All of this was strange and questionable behavior for any upstanding citizen of nineteenth-century New England, and even more so for a man once the head of arguably the most well-known Congregational Church in the United States. But what was at the root of Murray's behavior? There is no evidence that Murray conducted himself in such manner when it came to women in the earlier parts of his adult life. The late 1870s and early 1880s were certainly tumultuous times for Murray, given his separation from Park Street Church, the failure of the church at the Boston Music Hall, his financial ruin, and his formal separation from his first wife. Perhaps this unrest triggered the unorthodox behavior? Many people who have their lives turned upside down in so many facets at once exhibit previously unthinkable behavior. Murray might have found solace and distraction from the failings of his life in scandalous behavior with the young women.

Another possibility is presented by the rising, progressive free love movement. This nineteenth-century movement differed from its eponymous counterpart of the late 1960s and early 1970s. While the latter focused on casual sex and lack of commitment, the former was a movement toward free choice of monogamous partners and freedom to end marriage when love dissipated.[20] Presidential candidate Victoria Woodhull summarized the movement's ethos in this way: "Yes, I am a Free Lover. I have an inalienable, constitutional and natural right to love whom I may, to love as long or as short a period as I can; to change that love every day if I please, and with that right neither you nor any law you can frame have any right to interfere."[21] Rather than promiscuity, the freedom sought by these nineteenth-century men and women was the freedom to commit to whomever they chose, regardless of legal or economic conditions. Many in the movement sought to separate the state from sexual matters such as marriage, birth control, and adultery.[22]

In addition to marriage reform and birth control, the free love movement embraced issues such as marital rape, rejection of public authority, dress reform, health reform, divorce reform, spiritualism, and even environmental conservation. In his seminal 1977 study of the nineteenth-century free love movement, *The Sex Radicals: Free Love in High Victorian America*, Hal Sears states that "free love simply allowed no coercion in sexual relations, whether from the legally prescribed duties of marriage or from the unrestricted urgings of libido."[23] Coercion here included coercion from church and state.

While Murray's preaching and many facets of his personal life were often unorthodox by the conservative standards of Park Street Church, a good deal of evidence points to his involvement, at least for a time, with the free love movement. The most direct evidence comes from Murray's own words, or at least words attributed to the controversial minister. In the October 17, 1883, edition of *The Orleans Republican*, a newspaper published in Albion, New York, Murray is quoted as saying that he "is now a free-thinker and a believer in easy divorce" and that his "professions and practices are now made to harmonize."[24] *The Orleans Republican* made a point of explaining to its readers that "easy divorce" was "another name for free love."[25]

Like most topics, Murray was not afraid to espouse his views on divorce in the public forum. He gave several public lectures titled "American Divorce," in which he advocated for easy divorce. An article in the October 8, 1883, edition of *The New York Herald* recounted one such lecture:

> The audience that filled Chickering Hall last evening to hear Mr. W. H. H. Murray lecture upon "American Divorce" listened with unmistakable signs of attentive interest. Mr. Murray's delivery was rather too rapid, his gestures few and unstudied, and there was no attempt at oratorical effect, but his rhetoric brought out frequent and spontaneous applause.[26]

The *New York Herald* article explained that Murray believed there were presently two parties on divorce in America. The first party, referred to by Murray as the Church Party, believed that divorce should be granted only for "scriptural causes": adultery and desertion. The second party, which Murray dubbed the Popular Party, advocated divorce for a multitude of causes.[27]

Murray asserted that "marriage today is a practical, not an ideal matter," and "divorce is as practical a question as marriage."[28] Marriage and divorce, Murray told his audience, were matters for the legislature and the courts, not the church. He followed that assertion with a strong statement in favor of individual determination: "Marriage and divorce are personal matters, and the making or annulment of the marriage contract must be largely left to the affection, the judgment and the good sense of the parties themselves."[29]

Finally, Murray asserted in his "American Divorce" lecture that divorce was not too common in America.[30] He believed that the reason for the growing liberalization of divorce laws in America was the increasing recognition of the equal rights of women. Women needed liberal divorce laws to enable them to escape the cruelty, drunkenness, abuse, and neglect of their husbands. It is not hard to imagine the intemperance of Dickinson Murray, and his ill treatment of W. H. H. Murray's mother Sally that his friend Joseph Cook hints at,[31] influencing the young Murray toward this more liberal approach toward divorce.

As he had many times before, Murray sought to place his progressive lectures on divorce in a more permanent, written form. Before his death, he penned a manuscript titled "A Handbook on Marriage and Divorce."[32] A planned public announcement of the work contained the following description:

> W. H. H. Murray has just completed a volume in the preparation of which he has been engaged for twenty five years. . . . It is a clean and clear cut treatise of this much vexed and befogged subject and stands in style and statement in sharp contrast to the pious platitudes and careless statements that so largely of late constitute the so called discussion of the "divorce question" in our country.[33]

In this unpublished work, Murray explained his views on the topic. On marriage, he wrote:

> The method by which marriage is consummated is a civil contract. This view applied to the English speaking race wherever found. The chiefest characteristic of the contract—the one thing that constitutes it—is that it expresses the voluntary action of the parties that are united in any form of association with it. The marriage contract then, is the result of voluntary action of the man and woman united by it unassisted or influenced by any outside party. The law cannot make this contract for them. The church cannot make it. No outside party or parties, however associated or under whatever name, with any pretense of power or holiness can marry a man or a woman.[34]

As a civil contract, marriage to Murray was a state entered into because both husband and wife expected to receive benefits from it:

The marriage originates in the hope of benefit, of peace, of happiness, of life long blessing and without this hope it would never be formed and on the fulfillment of this reasonable hope and formative expectation, the marriage contract rests. If this hope fails, if this expectation is not realized, if not blessing but reverse flows from the contract, then a state of things exists that was not anticipated when the contract was conceived and consummated and the parties are brought face to face with an altogether different question, namely whether the annulment of the contract is not feasible and, in some instances, whether it is not a duty, resting equally upon both parties to unite in its annulment.[35]

In noting the religious intrusion into the realm of the civil contract, Murray wrote:

It was not until Christianity had become a State religion and had consolidated its temporal power, made itself secure with vast revenues and had had the time to foster superstition and make gross ignorance universal with kings, princes and people alike that marriage was ever regarded as anything but a civil contract solely under the control of civil law.[36]

Murray expanded the liberal view of divorce he espoused in his lecture for readers of his handbook. He insisted that he did not believe that "a single case of divorcement between husband and wife can be produced which did injustice to the individual or brought evil to the community."[37]

Addressing critics of divorce, Murray wrote:

But to say that the foundations of the family are being dangerously shaken by reason of the multiplicity of divorces is not true; and the parties who are making such assertions and multiplying clamor through the public journals and pulpits that always become noisy over any new subject that is unable to secure local notoriety are not credited by the country at large. . . .

Divorce is not a disease but a remedy for a disease—the unhappy marriage.[38]

Echoing many tenets of the free love movement, Murray praised American women and advocates for their right to divorce, as well as to be free of the expectations of child rearing and submissive marriages. He wrote that child rearing was not the primary object of marriage. Murray asserted rather that "the first object of marriage was companionship, mental and spiritual; entertainment and the uplifting which comes from these. The second object was the propagation of the species."[39] He continued:

Indeed Governments and the Church has looked upon women primarily as breeders. The one has given pecuniary reward to and the other has pronounced blessings on the woman who bore the most children. Thus making a travesty on the holiest function known to the Earth.

The wife is not primarily a breed to the man any more than she is primarily an animal. She is primarily a spirit, a companion, a solace, a comfort, a helpmeet. And these high offices—the highest known in human relationship can all be fulfilled by a woman to a man without bearing a child to him.[40]

Murray held American women at the zenith of their sex and therefore as wise to the erroneous views of marriage and divorce that conservative society pushed upon them:

Such women will not put up with what the women of other countries will condone. They are fully aware that marriage is a civil contract—how with their intelligence can they be ignorant of it—and that the essence of a contract is mutual obligation between those making it. They know they have the right to claim respect and respectful treatment, and naturally resent brutal treatment. They do not recognize that an unmurmuring submission to kicks and blows of drunken husbands is evidence of wifely dutifulness or that they are called upon to remain as mistress in a house whose rooms are filled with cursing and profanity.

It is because the American woman, is intelligent, courageous and sweet enough to make the noblest of wives and the best of mothers that she declines to accept hell for heaven or a lie for a sacrament.[41]

So was Murray an advocate of the free love movement? It appears likely that he was. As a literary denizen of Boston and frequent visitor to New York City, he would have been exposed to the movement's leaders and propositions. One of the more popular free love papers of the time, *The Word*,[42] was published in Cambridge, Massachusetts, and Murray almost certainly would have been aware of *The Word* and other similar controversial publications.

In addition to being in the right circles and the right geographical area to be exposed to the tenets of free love, many of Murray's actions and words are congruent with those principles. Murray's separation and eventual divorce from his wife Isadora speaks to the former minister's belief that marriage could and should be ended by the individuals involved without the need for sanction from the church.

If the *Orleans Republican* report is to be believed, Murray stated that he was a freethinker and believed in easy divorce, one of the foundations of the free love movement. This admission is made more credible by Murray's "American Divorce" lectures, in which he advocated the free love movement's approach to practical divorce laws to ensure the rights of women. Finally, Murray's various relationships with his "daughters" and other women indicate that his views toward women, marriage, and sex were far from traditional.

Chapter 15

Lake Champlain

I desired, furthermore, to commend this lake to the favor of the American people, not only because of its historic connections but because while it stands at present comparatively unoccupied, it nevertheless supplies to them, for the purpose of recreation, one of the most desirable pleasure resorts of the country.

—W. H. H. Murray, *Lake Champlain*

During his residence in Burlington, Murray devoted a large amount of energy advocating for the sport of yachting on Lake Champlain. In 1886, he went so far as to deliver an address to a special meeting of Burlington businessmen concerning yachting and the opportunities presented by nearby Lake Champlain.[1]

Instead, Murray pursued this advocacy for the virtues of Lake Champlain throughout his time in Vermont with the vigor and persistence that marked all of his passions. During this time, he is credited with "calling attention to the broad expanse of lake opposite Burlington that had not been used as it might be by sail and hulls of modern cut."[2]

Murray was particularly intent on promoting the use of the sharpie class of sailboat on the lake's waters. The sharpie was a type of oyster boat developed for use on the Long Island Sound, a body of water Murray was intimately familiar with from his youth in Guilford and his college days in New Haven. According to Murray, the sharpies were "well adapted to meet the wants of amateurs, and will do more to make yachting a popular recreation to a degree never hitherto realized."[3]

In *The Migrations of an American Boat Type,* author Howard I. Chapelle explains that "the sharpie yacht was introduced on Lake Champlain in the late 1870s by Rev. W. H. H. Murray. . . . The hull of the Champlain sharpie retained most of the characteristics of the New Haven hull, but the Champlain boats were fitted with a wide variety of rigs, some highly experimental. A few commercial sharpies were built at Burlington, Vermont, for hauling produce on the lake, but most of the sharpies built there were yachts."[4]

To promote the use of the sharpie on Lake Champlain, Murray and local businessmen had a sharpie boat built for demonstration purposes. The boat was christened *Burlington* and was owned by the yacht club.[5] Murray also had his own sharpie class boat, which he named *Champlain,* constructed in Connecticut and brought to Burlington.[6] The *Champlain* was forty feet long and had a beam of nine feet.[7] The sailing of the *Burlington* and the *Champlain* on the lake had its desired effect, and in quick order, many similar sailing vessels were built and sailed on the lake.

Murray later described his sharpie *Champlain* in an article written for *Outing Magazine:*

> The yacht Champlain is no fancy boat, although a pretty enough one to look at if one has an eye for good lines, shapely proportions and a handy rig, and as it has stood the test of cruising by day and night in difficult waters with credit, carries its own indorsement with those who love a safe and easily-handled boat. Briefly put, the Champlain is of sharpie model with thirty feet water line and the customary overhang of the sharpies. Her sides amidships are cut away so that the angle of flare is very pronounced. From this feature she loses, of course, something of initial stability and goes down in a good breeze readily to her gunwale line, but there she gets to her bearings and there remains sturdily, being assisted thereto by the size and weight of her loaded centreboard. The sharpies and cutters have a resemblance in this, that they sail their fastest when pressed over to an angle of sharper decline than boats of broader beam and greater initial stability could safely be carried.[8]

Characteristically, Murray did not hesitate to advocate for his chosen craft or his preferred method of sailing:

I do not know how many yachtsmen who may read these lines belong to the fraternity of cruisers, but those who do will bear me out in the statement that nothing so educates a skipper or brings out the strong and weak points of a yacht as a good long cruise. Harbor sailing is delightful, and a race between well-matched rival boats is very spirited; but for downright enjoyment, with a goodly amount of education thrown in gratis, I know of nothing in yachting experience that can compare with prolonged cruising. He who slips his moorings for a cruise of thirty, sixty or, better yet, ninety days will bring home with him a good many reminiscences of his voyaging of a nature which a lifetime of sailing on familiar waters cannot give him.[9]

Murray, of course, could not write such an article without sharing a personal adventure with *Outing*'s readers:

I recall a run made by the Champlain on the lower St. Lawrence, in returning from a cruise to the Saguenay some years ago. We passed Baie St. Paul in the evening, whirled along by a rising gale blowing directly up the river. The night was pitchy dark, the tide running fiercely on the ebb at the rate of five miles an hour at the least. The water was very wild, as one can easily imagine. Stemming such a current it would not do to shorten sail if one wished to pass Cape Tourmente and get into quiet water between the Isle of Orleans and the north shore, so we let every sail stand, cleated the sheets tightly, and let her drive. How she did tear onward! The froth and spume lay deep on her pathways and after deck. The waves crested fiercely, rolling against the current, and the black water broke into phosphor as we slashed through it. I do not recall that I ever saw a yacht forced along more savagely. How the water roared under the ledges and along the rough shores of Tourmente! And I was profoundly grateful when we were able to bear off to starboard and run into the still water back of Orleans. Perhaps that midnight cup of coffee did not taste well! Its heat ran through my chilled veins like Chartreuse. I can taste it yet![10]

Murray's advocacy for yachting on Lake Champlain culminated in the establishment of the Sharpie Yacht Club of Burlington later in 1886.[11] The Sharpie Yacht Club quickly morphed into the Lake Champlain Yacht Club. The constitution, bylaws, and sailing regulations of the original club were finalized and signed on May 16, 1887, and the club survives to this day. The initial roster of club officers included W. Boerum Wetmore as commodore and W. A. Crombie as vice commodore. Murray was a member of the club's executive committee.[12] Among the initial two hundred members of the club were sailors from as far south as Albany and New York City. Many members were wealthy individuals who had summer homes along the New York and Vermont shores of the lake.

That Murray's advocacy for yachting on Lake Champlain gave rise to the Lake Champlain Yacht Club, and the sport in general on the great northern lake, is undisputed. A contemporary report on the founding of the club states, "Everyone agrees that the present yacht club is the outcome of his earlier efforts, although it has outgrown what he developed and contended for at the first."[13]

~

Murray's residence near the shores of Lake Champlain also gave him occasion to observe the various forms of wildlife that frequented that aquatic habitat. These observations included the vaunted Lake Champlain Monster, now locally known as "Champy."[14] Stories of the legendary sea serpent date back to before European settlement of Lake Champlain's shores.

It is not surprising, then, that the former minister reported his own sighting of the serpent while he lived in Burlington. In a report to the *New York Times* dated May 22, 1887, Murray recounted his observation of the monster.[15] Murray recalled being drawn from his house by an excited crowd that had gathered along the shore. Upon investigation, he found that the great serpent had been spotted in the bay. While listening to a member of the crowd report what he had seen, Murray was granted with a sighting of his own:

> And sure enough, right in front me not two miles away, the lake being scarcely rippled, the air clear as plate glass, I beheld the sea serpent, and I must say the spectacle was a most startling one. . . . In length he seemed 100 feet longer than a canal boat would at that distance. His color was at times a slaty brown, at

others a glistening white like the scales of a shad. His motion was undulatory, and a kind of quivering through his whole length characterized him. He moved with astonishing rapidity toward the north, and when he was showing his full length of his appearance he sank from sight. . . . The coolest observer, the most skeptical, would have been perfectly convinced that his eyes had beheld a sea monster.[16]

When the serpent disappeared from sight, Murray had the foresight, and apparently the time, to retrieve a field glass from his house. Returning to the crowd along the shore, Murray was blessed with a second observation of the legendary monster:

And sure enough there was the serpent once more, white and sheeny, moving with immense rapidity, with the same peculiar vibratory motion. I brought my glass to bear on him instantly and the mystery was in that instant solved. The immense sea monster at once resolved itself into several hundreds of small birds, of the plover family, flying in a long line which swung up and down and to the right and to the left as they flew. The underside of the wings and breasts were snowy white; their backs were slaty brown.[17]

Thus, at least in the eyes of Murray, the age-old mystery of the Lake Champlain monster was solved.

~

Amid unmasking sea monsters and starting a yacht club, Murray also found time to write while living in Burlington. In 1888, he published his third book, *Daylight Land*, a story of four gentlemen (including Murray) traveling by rail across Canada.[18] Of why he wrote *Daylight Land*, Murray stated:

The prompting motive in the preparation of Daylight Land was this: The little book "Adventures in the Wilderness" was published in 1868, I think . . . I had no thought at that time of becoming an author. The several chapters of that little volume were written as exercises in composition. I was, at the writing of the book, only some twenty-six years old. I knew little of life or nature, and absolutely nothing of what literary balance and fitness mean. Naturally, the book, because of the fame it won, became, as years passed, my knowledge grew apace and my powers of expression ripened, a regret to me. It did not represent me as an author.[19]

In 1890, Murray released his most literary and, perhaps, abstract work, *Mamelons and Ungava, a Legend of Saguenay*.[20] The collection featured the character John Norton the Trapper and took place among mystical native peoples in northern Quebec, Canada. *Mamelons* had been previously released in 1888 under the title *The Doom of Mamelons*,[21] but it was now joined with its sister work, *Ungava*. The two stories were part of a planned six part "Canadian Idyls" by the author.

After *Mamelons and Ungava*, the author's focus again turned to his natural surroundings, and Murray penned a small volume on Lake Champlain and its history. *Lake Champlain and Its Shores*, published in 1890, was Murray's fourth full-length book.[22]

~

Lake Champlain and Its Shores is a relatively short work. Murray begins the book with a prefatory chapter on the outdoor life in general—again praising the virtues of time spent outdoors. The author then goes on to explore the history of Lake Champlain, advocate for the establishment of a national park, and boast of the yachting opportunities presented by the lake.

Murray's treatment of the history of Lake Champlain and his advocacy for the establishment of a national park are perhaps the most interesting components of the volume. Murray begins his history of Lake Champlain by recounting the numerous explorers who visited North America before the lake's namesake, Samuel de Champlain. He wrote of the Norsemen sailors, the Cabots from Venice, and Henry Hudson.[23]

Murray then wrote of Champlain's discovery of the lake and encounters with Native Americans, as well as the subsequent battles fought on the waters. He traces the success of many of the leaders of the Revolutionary War and War of 1812 to their early trials on Lake Champlain:

In what school was Schuyler of New York trained? Where did Putnam of Connecticut learn to fight? Where did the grit of Stark from New Hampshire gets its razor edge? Whence came the cannon that manned the works of Washington on Dorchester Heights and enabled him to drive the British out of Boston? Fighting against who and where did New England and New York men learn the use of arms, the habits of obedience, the coolness of veterans under fire, and that indifference to numbers which more than once held the Revolutionary army together and made it formidable to its foe? Here it was, here on Lake Champlain and its connecting waters, that the men who fought so bravely under Prescott, Putnam, Stark, Gates and Washington learned the lesson of war and from it, as a martial school, graduated as veterans for the Revolutionary struggle.[24]

Murray's discussion of Fort Ticonderoga and Benedict Arnold bears mentioning here. In retelling the capture of the fort by Ethan Allen, Murray impresses upon the reader his conviction that, contrary to accepted history, Arnold was not with Allen during the raid and did not arrive at Fort Ticonderoga until days after its capture by the revolutionary forces.[25] Relying on testimony from Allen's guide Nathan Beman, who was by Allen's side throughout the raid on the fort, Murray concludes that Arnold was not present during its capture. This conclusion contradicts the widely accepted historical accounts of the endeavor and may simply be the result of a well-known boaster paying homage to an even more famous blusterer.

Once the history of Lake Champlain is laid out by Murray in *Lake Champlain and Its Shores*, the author dedicates a chapter to advocate for the establishment of a great national park. The boundaries of this national park would be vast, spanning from Niagara Falls to Acadia:

If the reader will take a map of the country, and, beginning with Niagara Falls draw a line eastward to Mount Desert Island, and with this as the central line, construct a parallelogram, he will have embraced within it such a grouping of natural scenery both as regards sublimity and beauty, along with such a multitude of resources for human recreation and entertainment, as may not be found elsewhere in connection, either on this continent or in Europe.[26]

Murray goes on to discuss the natural wonders contained within the marked area, including Niagara Falls, the Thousand Islands, the Adirondacks, Lake Champlain, Lake George, Ausable Chasm, the Green Mountains, the White Mountains, Bar Harbor, and Mount Desert. Murray knew that the declaration of such a vast territory as a national park would be unfathomable, but he wrote of this area as a great national park in spirit:

> Congress may resolve and newspaper correspondents may with hasty pen declare that this or that spot, distinguished by some local phenomena, shall be known as the National Park, but neither formal resolution nor hasty verdict of casual writers can change the geography of the continent or the facts of nature; and these declare—and with an emphasis that cannot be misunderstood or unheeded by the intelligent—that the *Great National Park, for the whole American people,* lies with the lines of the parallelogram I have suggested, and to it there is not now, and never can be, on the continent, a rival.[27]

The final component of *Lake Champlain and Its Shores* concerns further advocacy of the sport of yachting on Lake Champlain. Murray viewed inland yachting as a safer and more desirable alternative to that taking place on the magnificent, but extremely dangerous, oceans. Murray cited North America as the only civilized continent that provided sailors the opportunity to sail four or five thousand miles of inland waters without going over the same course twice.[28]

The author viewed Lake Champlain as the natural starting point for the preparation necessary for such extended aquatic excursions. "It is the only lake in all this east country of ours that can serve as a school in which practical knowledge of yachts and yachting can be taught," Murray wrote.[29] "It is, moreover, so placed as to be easily accessible from the great, seaboard cities, from which the majority of our true tourists and sportsmen come."[30]

Much like his treatment of the Adirondack Mountains in *Adventures in the Wilderness*, Murray provided practical guidance with respect to yachting on Lake Champlain within the pages of his 1890 book. He described in detail the many coves and islands of the lake, as well as the shallows and shoals that posed dangers to the yachtsman. For example, his sailing directions for Shelburne Bay included the following:

> Two miles of safe sailing; free of reefs. North of the mouth of this bay, near the centre of the entrance, a half-mile to the

north, is Proctor's Reef; buoy on northwest corner. Can sail near the buoy, but give a quarter mile margin if you go to the south of it.[31]

~

At some point in 1890, word reached Murray that the Murray Homestead and surrounding lands in Guilford were again available for purchase. The five years in Burlington had seen a resurgence of sorts for Murray, with respect to lectures and book sales, and the timing of this news was fortuitous. Eager to bring his second wife and young daughters to Connecticut, Murray made arrangements to purchase the homestead. His time in Burlington had come to an end.

In 1891, at the age of fifty-one, W. H. H. Murray brought his wife Frances and his two daughters, Maud and Ruby, home to Guilford. This would be the family's last move. It is easy to imagine his pleasure and excitement at having reclaimed the homestead once lost to his creditors and brought his new family to his ancestral home along Long Island Sound.

For reasons unknown, the Murrays did not move into the homestead immediately upon their arrival in Guilford in 1891. Instead, for nearly two years, Murray and his family lived in the Charles Frances House northwest of the homestead.[32] This was the house that had previously served as the headquarters of the Murray Stock Farm.

While the Murrays lived in the Charles Frances House, Frances gave birth to the couple's third child. On August 6, 1892, Grace Norton Murray was born. A year after Grace's birth, circumstances were right for the family of five to move into the original Murray Homestead. At the age of fifty-three, W. H. H. Murray, with his wife and three daughters, returned home.

Frances Rivers Murray.

W. H. H. Murray.

W. H. H. Murray and Maud Murray.

Frances Murray and daughters.

Ethel Murray.

Ethel and Ruby Murray.

Grace Murray.

Maud Murray.

Ethel Murray as Joan of Arc.

PART FOUR

HOME

Chapter 16

Home and Family

Ah, friends, dear friends, as years go on and heads get gray—how fast the guests do go! Touch hands, touch hands with those that stay.

—W. H. H. Murray, *Holiday Tales*

What turned out to be the final decade of W. H. H. Murray's colorful life, 1894 through 1904, was markedly different from the preceding fifty-four years. These last ten years saw Murray settle down in the regained Murray Homestead. From the house in Guilford, now bereft of the once-impressive accoutrements of his stock farm, Murray quietly managed his publishing affairs, traveled for lectures, including at least one stop on the Chautauqua tour in the Connecticut River Valley at Laurel Park on July 20, 1898, during which Murray delivered a lecture advocating for a continental-focused national policy rather than what he viewed as increasing imperialistic policies in the United States,[1] and tended to his growing family.

Murray took great pride in the family he raised with Frances Rivers Murray. Maud Marguerite Murray was the eldest daughter, born on June 8, 1887, when Bill and Frances lived in Burlington, Vermont. There is no record of the origin of Maud's middle name, but its commonality with that of Murray's "daughter" Fannie Bursley, also known as F. Marguerita Murray, cannot go unnoticed.

Ruby Rivers Murray was the next child born to Bill and Frances. This second daughter was born in 1888 just before the family moved from Burlington to Guilford. A letter from Murray, who wrote from the

Parker House in Boston, dated November 12, 1890, expresses his devotion to his new family:

> My dear Little Angel
>
> Your letter which kind Mamma sent to me is received and it made me very happy to get it. I am glad that you are well and good and kind to dear sister. Poor Papa wishes to come home very much and take you in his arms and kiss you many times. I hope to come home pretty soon and to bring you and sister, Mamma and Marguerita some nice presents so we can all be happy together. Good night sweet one and remember that you are Papa's dear little blessing.
>
> Lovingly yours,
>
> Father[2]

Murray's inclusion of Marguerita in his remembrances to his daughter indicates that either Marguerita was still living near the family or visiting them around this time.

Three years after Ruby's birth, on August 6, 1892, Frances gave birth to a third daughter, Grace Norton Murray. Finally, the family was completed on December 20, 1896, with the birth of Ethel Esther Murray. She was the only one of the four daughters to have been born in the same room of the house in which her father had been born some fifty-six years before.

If W. H. H. Murray was ever disappointed by the lack of a son, no indication of such disappointment survives. Instead, the written record evidences a fierce devotion between father and daughters. Murray took an active part in the raising of his four girls, culminating in his writing of his final book, a volume to explain how he was educating his daughters.[3]

Chapter 17

How I Am Educating My Daughters

The system in vogue has been accurately if inelegantly defined as the "System of Cram"! Facts, figures, names, dates, rules and a hodge-podge of book knowledge are literally *crammed* into them.

—W. H. H. Murray

Convinced that the Guilford public school was inadequate for the task of educating his four daughters, Murray took it upon himself to teach them. He provided daily instruction based on a plan of education he thought best fit for his girls. Not surprisingly, Murray placed his highest priority on the instruction of the English language and wanted his girls to master that medium:

> I regard the English language as the most facile and noblest medium of expressing human thought and feeling ever used on earth. He who knows how to write and speak the English language in purity, with correctness and finished forcefulness, must be admitted to be a scholar of the highest rank. And he who cannot do this, no matter to what other knowledge he has come, lacks the cultivation of finished scholarship.[1]

So convinced was Murray in his ability to provide the girls a better education that he set his educational philosophy in type and, in 1900, published his last book, aptly titled *How I Am Educating My Daughters*. Within that volume, Murray wrote that the object of educating young minds was to foster four types of love: love of parents, love of home, love of God, and love of the nation.[2] He found fault in the public educational system's failure to educate a child as a child:

> The great objection to the system of educating children now in vogue among us is that it does not educate. And the reason that it does not educate is because it is not based on a right understanding of child nature or what education really is. The child as a child is not considered. The pupils are treated rather as little men and women and forced to adjust themselves to rules, methods of study, and an environment not natural or pleasant to them.[3]

Objections to education in America were not new to Murray. In several of his published sermons, Murray, as minister, had attacked the failures of education. Murray particularly criticized the education of young girls: "We educate our girls to spend, and not to earn; to depend upon others for support, and not upon themselves."[4] Insisting that the preparation of young women by the common schools are inadequate, he proclaimed:

> For eight years—years which cover the formative period of her life—you give her the best advantages of your superb public schools. . . . For eight years you have been educating her to love ease and refinement, and all the concomitants of such a state. . . . You have made her a queen; now guarantee her a throne. What can she do?[5]

Here again, with his stance on education, Murray reflected a growing progressivism within education reform circles. The progressive education movement in America, led by such nineteenth-century men as John Dewey and Colonel Frances W. Parker, was largely an offspring of the European Romanticism that had traversed the Atlantic Ocean.[6] The progressives sought a more child-centered education system, with thinkers such as Emerson and Thoreau urging the merits of an education based on the qualities of village life and nature.[7] The educational reform movement in America was made possible by changes in family size, in new gender roles within an expanding bourgeois culture, and in the softening of religious orthodoxy within Protestantism.[8]

Promoters of reform assailed the dominance of memorization, textbooks, and physical discipline in American schools. As Reese writes: "Teachers everywhere frequently spent most of their time drilling children in the basic subjects. A foreign visitor to several New York City schools in the 1890s was struck by the heavy reliance on memorization: "I heard in one class the boys get up one after another recording the names, dates and chief performances of the eighteen presidents of the United States."[9] Opposed to this, the progressives proclaimed that "children were active, not passive, learners; that children were innocent and good, not fallen; that women, not men, best reared and educated the young; that early education, without question, made all the difference; that nature, and not books alone, was perhaps the best teacher; that kindness and benevolence, not stern discipline and harsh rebukes, should reign in the home and the classroom; and, finally, that the curriculum needed serious reform, to remove the vestiges of medievalism."[10]

Reflecting the progressive approach to educating children, Murray believed in a more Socratic-like method of teaching. He wrote:

> Education is not the acquisition of knowledge but the development of natural faculty. To enlarge and quicken the affections, to strengthen memory, to develop the reason, enable the pupil to think clearly and express himself or herself accurately and forcibly; to qualify him to fully concentrate his mind at any moment of time, under all conditions of place and circumstance, on one particular subject and by so doing decide and act rightly and efficiently; this is the object of education. And beyond this there is none other. The system that does this is a success. If it does not do it, it is a failure.[11]

Again, Murray's homeschool philosophy and regimen was laid out in detail within the pages of *How I Am Educating My Daughters*. In the first pages of the volume, the author included a quote from his contemporary and friend Henry Ward Beecher: "Our children are God's children, not ours only, and given us to train for him. As their Teachers, we teach ourselves more than we teach them."[12]

Not surprisingly, Murray, as a former minister, devotes a great many words to the spiritual development of his children. In this, he stresses living their lives in the Christian example over strict religious study, again revealing the evolution of Murray's theological stance. Murray wrote: "Of dogma and formulated creeds, of ritualistic observance, of human interpretation of the Master's self-interpreting words, they [his daughters] know nothing. Nor would they miss much, in my opinion, if they never should."[13] These words further evidence Murray's turn from old-school theology and its dogma toward a more progressive spirituality.

In addition to spiritual education, Murray explained the lessons in English, mathematics, politics, literature, civics, chess playing, the outdoors, and home life that he imparted to his daughters. With respect to love of country, He wrote of instilling not only national pride but also sincere knowledge in his daughters. The four girls were instructed to learn both the Declaration of Independence and the Constitution by memory.[14]

Murray also placed strong emphasis on family within his education program. He believed that the institution of the family in the United States was in great jeopardy. Murray wrote that the family institution must be reformed and renewed within itself. "Children must be regarded as the most precious gifts given of heaven," the former minister wrote. "Compared with them wealth is of no value, and social pleasures of no account."[15]

To help revitalize the American family, Murray advocated an hour of dedicated family time each day.[16] This hour was critical to the both the love within the family and the children's education. He concluded:

It has become the center and central source of joy and helping to the family life. Mentally and affectionally it is the greatest factor for good in the household. It is the school of literature, of manners, and of unconventional piety to us all. It is devoted to entertainment, wit, humor, anecdote, storytelling, recitations, scripture reading, games fun and frolic. All that can entertain healthy, clever children are incorporate in it.[17]

Murray's friend H. J. Griswold sheds light on his friend's relationship with his family, writing that Murray "has brought up a family of four lovely and promising daughters, to whom he was more of a companion than parent, whose education he undertook and directed, with whom he roamed the woodlands and fields teaching them to speak and write the English language with the same correctness and finished forcefulness that characterized his own speech and writings."[18]

∾

How I Am Educating My Daughters was the last book that Murray would write. It was first published in 1900, with a second edition released in 1902.[19] After completing the book, Murray spent the first years of the new century with his family at the Murray Homestead. He attended to his daughters' education and spent time with his wife Frances. The homestead was allowed to deteriorate during these years, as Murray seemed less concerned with the material health of his home than the spiritual and mental health of his family.

By 1902, Murray's own health, like his property, had deteriorated. He apparently suffered from kidney ailments.[20] His days were quiet ones. It is said that he was happy during these years, "simply resting amid the surroundings of his youthful aspirations and his heart's desire. Here after his experience with the world's storms, he found a haven of peace."[21]

William Henry Harrison Murray died peacefully surrounded by his wife and four daughters on March 3, 1904. His death came just over a month before his sixty-fourth birthday. Completing a full circle, Murray died at the Murray Homestead in the small room just off of the kitchen—the same room in which he was born. His daughter Ruby reported that his final words were "that life had been so full of good things for him and that if the next world held only half the sweetness and delight of this one, he would be well content."[22]

~

That Murray had taken the education of his daughters seriously is indicated not only by the book he dedicated to the subject but also by the success his daughters enjoyed later in life. By all accounts, all four daughters led happy, fulfilled lives, with various degrees of adventure thrown in for good measure.

Maud, W. H. H. Murray's eldest child, left Guilford, Connecticut, after finishing high school and attended the Metropolitan Training School on Blackwell's Island[23] in New York City. The school trained nurses and was affiliated with the Metropolitan Hospital. Maud subsequently attended Drew Seminary in Carmel, New York, and the Quincy Mansion School in Wollaston, Massachusetts. Later, she married Reverend Annesley Thomas Young, known by most as Dr. Young. An Episcopalian, he had been a chaplain at Blackwell's Island.[24] He served for many years as pastor of the Church of the Advent in Chicago.[25] Maud and Dr. Young had one child, Frances Caroline Young, but the child lived less than twenty-four hours.

Dr. Young died at the age of sixty-nine in 1942. Maud returned to the Murray Homestead following her husband's death and lived there alone until her own death on November 28, 1978. She is buried, together with Dr. Young and their daughter Frances, next to her father.

Ruby appears to have been the daughter who excelled academically the most. She obtained a master's degree in chemistry from Mount Holyoke College in 1914 and completed her doctorate in chemistry at Cornell University in 1916.[26] She worked as a research chemist at Cornell from 1916 to 1918.[27] In June 1918, Ruby married John Caleb Orcutt, a banker.[28] The Orcutts raised four boys, and Ruby completed her career as a chemist at Columbia University in New York, working there from 1934 to 1936.[29] She died on April 7, 1976,[30] and was buried with her husband in Pawlet, Vermont.

Grace was another independent soul. After her father's death, Grace, like her sisters, attended Guilford High School. After graduating, Grace attended the Leland Powers School in Boston, from which she graduated in 1915.[31] She then studied drama for a year in New York City. Returning to Connecticut, Grace served as the organizer of the Fairfield County Women's Suffrage Organization from 1917 to 1920[32] and later the organizer of the Connecticut League of Women Voters.[33] During World War I, Grace was a speaker for the State Council of Defense, for which she was one of seven women from Connecticut to receive a certificate of commendation from the National Council of Defense in Washington, D.C.[34] Later, she was appointed to the position of mercantile inspector at the Connecticut State Labor Department.[35] She married Charles Ernest Williamson,[36] a leader in the Fairfield County Republican party.[37] Her brother-in-law Dr. Young married the couple.[38] Grace and Charles had two children and are, like Maud, buried near W. H. H. Murray on the grounds of the Murray Homestead.

Ethel, the youngest of the four daughters, was a mere eight years old when her father died. Her lack of years with her father probably contributed to the rather wild turns her life took in her younger years. Leaving Connecticut, Ethel went to New York City. There, she attended the New York School of Dramatic Art and, under the stage name Glory Mora, became a member of the Winter Garden Company[39] and the production of the *Passing Show*, a stage show designed to compete with the *Ziegfeld Follies*. It was likely in this role that she met young Thomas Coffing Beach, the son of a wealthy businessman from Hartford.

Tom and Ethel enjoyed a brief, whirlwind courtship. The brevity seemed to raise the concern of Frances, who wrote Ethel about the prospect of marrying Tom:

Dear Baby

I don't know what Maude wrote you or what she got from you by telegram last eve, as I feel sure it was from you. But as for me—I don't wish you to marry "B" unless he can tell you how much you will have to live on. Of course his father is a rich man but it will be some time before T gets his share of it; and you are far too young and good looking to throw yourself away. If you will just wait a little and keep straight as you have been doing, you will surely get some one more fitted to you.[40]

Despite this plea from her mother, Ethel married Tom in New York City on July 27, 1917.[41] Ethel was just twenty-one, and Tom was only seventeen. After their marriage, the couple resided in West Hartford, Connecticut, and, for a short while, on a Vermont farm purchased for the couple by Tom's father. The couple had two children: Charles Edward Beach II and Thomas Coffing Beach Jr.

In the fall of 1923, Ethel filed for divorce from Tom, alleging alienation of affections. Much to the chagrin of both the Murray and the Beach families, the divorce was quite public. Ethel sought support from Tom and sued his family for $350,000.[42] The matter appeared on the front page of the November 16, 1923, edition of the *Hartford Times*, accompanied by a large photograph of Ethel's previous appearance as a horse-riding Joan of Arc in a 1913 suffrage parade in Hartford.

Following her divorce, Ethel returned home to live at the Murray Homestead with her mother. Later, Ethel reportedly dated several men until finding the man who became her second husband, Milton Tenney MacDonald, known as Mac. Ethel and Mac were married on September 28, 1929.[43] The two had one child, Milton T. MacDonald Jr., born on January 28, 1934.[44] The couple settled in Georgetown, Connecticut, where Ethel lived for the rest of her life. She died on February 23, 1982, at the age of eighty-five and is buried with Mac in Massachusetts.[45]

≈

The death of Murray in 1904 left his wife Frances alone to raise the couple's four daughters. As a result of his many financial failures, the former preacher left his wife with substantial debt. As the foregoing reveals, as a widowed single parent, Frances was fairly successful: the Murray children all did well in life. Throughout Frances's remaining life, the four daughters kept in constant contact with their mother through frequent letters and visits. When they could afford to do so, each of the daughters would include gifts of money with their letters home. A census report in 1920 lists Frances as a sixty-one-year-old widowed farm operator.[46] She died on January 6, 1929, at the age of seventy and was buried next to her husband at the Murray Homestead.[47]

Afterword

The preceding pages endeavor to reveal the complexity of William Henry Harrison Murray. His was a life marked by continual flux. As a preacher, he swung from an orthodox, old-school theology to a more progressive ministry that emphasized action over dogma. This emphasis on action led Murray to his advocacy for the poor in Boston and other cities in America.

He embraced Muscular Christianity in the face of the physical, mental, and spiritual degradation he witnessed in the new, industrial, and urban society that emerged in the second half of the nineteenth century. Drawing on his experiences in the Adirondacks, Murray advocated time in nature for the members of the newly formed urban middle class who suffered the previously unencountered stresses of city life. In doing so, Murray democratized the retreats previously known only to the wealthy and fostered the concept of the vacation in America.

Murray's progressive attitudes at the pulpit, combined with his oversized character, allowed him to embrace elements of life that more conservative preachers shied from. Murray saw no discord among his love of God, horses, and the outdoors. He pursued each with equal vigor.

As a progressive thinker, Murray was in many ways out of sync with the cultural mainstream of the late nineteenth century, but he did reflect the growing movements of populism and progressivism that would come to a head in the early twentieth century. He advocated for the immigrant poor, the urban worker, and the middle class. He recognized the stress industrialization placed on the physical, mental, and spiritual well-being of a person and advocated restorative vacations in natural surroundings.

Murray believed that physical health went hand in hand with spiritual health. Throughout his life he was a steadfast proponent of temperance. Murray loathed the ill treatment of Native Americans and recognized the proud virtue of warriors such as Sitting Bull. He fought for more equitable divorce laws and the betterment of women within American society. Finally, in his later years, Murray recognized the weaknesses of public education, many of which survive today, and devised and wrote of an alternative approach to educating children.

Despite his original ministerial calling, Murray was anything but saintly. He was a constant self-promoter who continually sought wealth and fame. He deluded himself into believing he was a sharp businessman, regardless of his many financial failures. Murray was easily distracted, constantly pursuing one angle before quickly turning to the next.

As we have seen, after leaving the ministry, Murray entered a period of restlessness. His lack of a flock to lead, combined with numerous financial failures, sent him spinning through California, Texas, Montreal, and travel farther abroad. At the same time, he embraced the free love movement and subjected himself to continued scandal and ridicule in the public eye.

This restlessness ended in Montreal, where he met Frances Rivers. In his later years, Murray's declared trinity of passions—theology, horses, and the Adirondacks—morphed into his family, horses, and the natural wonders of North America. His zest for preaching to congregations in search of spiritual guidance was replaced by a fervent devotion to his wife and daughters. His love of the Adirondacks remained strong but fell within a broader category of admiration for all wonders of the natural environment he witnessed throughout North America. Still, Murray's love for horses held steady throughout his years.

While Murray might have preferred to achieve immortality through his efforts at his stock farm, or his later literary works, his most meaningful and lasting contribution was his advocacy of the outdoors and the value of vacation for the urban class. The easily read, funny, over-the-top, and, at times, simplistic *Adventures in the Wilderness; or, Camp-Life in the Adirondacks*, had a lasting impact on American culture. With that one volume, Murray introduced thousands of nineteenth-century Americans to the wonders of the natural world, its restorative power, and the joys of camping. Perhaps most significantly, Murray convinced the people they could do it too. By empowering his readers, William Henry Harrison Murray democratized the wilderness.

Yet, as this work has attempted to demonstrate, Murray was greater than his ode to the Adirondacks. He was a man of many passions, who constantly sought to share those passions with his fellow man, so convinced he was of their intrinsic worth. He was a man whose beliefs and values evolved with the tide of nineteenth-century progressivism, and in many ways Murray's life reflects the social reform movements that have shaped our modern society.

Books by W. H. H. Murray

Adventures in the Wilderness, Or Camp Life in the Adirondacks. Boston: Fields, Osgood, 1869.

Music Hall Sermons. Boston: Fields, Osgood, 1870.

Park Street Pulpit. Boston: James R. Osgood, 1871.

Words Fitly Spoken. Boston: Lee and Shepard, 1873.

The Perfect Horse. Boston: J. R. Osgood, 1873.

Deacons. Boston: Cupples and Hurd, 1874.

How Deacon Tubman & Parson Whitney Kept New Year's. Boston: Cupples and Hurd, 1887.

Daylight Land. Boston: Cupples and Hurd, 1888.

The Doom of Mamelons, a Legend of the Saguenay. Philadelphia: Hubbard Bros., 1888.

The Story That the Keg Told Me, and The Story of the Man Who Didn't Know Much. Boston: Cupples and Hurd, 1889.

Mamelons and Ungava. Boston: DeWolfe, Fiske, 1890.

Lake Champlain and Its Shores. Boston: DeWolfe, Fiske, 1890.

The Busted Ex-Texan and Other Stories. Boston: DeWolfe, Fiske, 1890.

How John Norton the Trapper Kept His Christmas. Boston: DeWolfe, Fiske, 1891.

Cones for the Campfire. Boston: DeWolfe, Fiske, 1891.

The Mystery of the Woods and the Man Who Missed It. Boston: DeWolfe, Fiske, 1891.

Holiday Tales. Springfield, MA: Springfield Printing and Binding, 1897.

Adirondack Tales Vols. I–V. Springfield, MA: Springfield Printing and Binding, 1897–98.

The Apple Tree's Easter or A Tale of Nature's Resurrection. Hartford: Case, Lockwood and Brainard, 1900.

How I am Educating My Daughters. Hartford: Case, Lockwood and Brainard, 1902.

Notes

Chapter 1. Guilford

1. "Historical Overview," Town of Guilford, accessed January 29, 2019, http://www.ci.guilford.ct.us/about-guilford/historical-overview/.

2. Kristen Nietering, Jordan Sorensen, and Mary Dunne, "A Short History of Guilford from Historic and Architectural Resources Inventory for the Town of Guilford, Connecticut Phase II Supplemental Survey" (Hartford: State of Connecticut, 2015).

3. Dickinson was one of three children of Calvin and Diadem (née Norton) Murray. His father, Calvin, died in 1810, when Dickinson was a young boy in an accident in which Calvin was smothered by charcoal.

4. "Mr. Murray's Stock Farm," *New York Sun*, August 6, 1879, 1.

5. Ibid.

6. Sally Munger Murray was the daughter of Chauncey and Jerusha (née Dowd) Munger. Like Calvin Murray, Chauncey Munger died in 1820, while his daughter was still young.

7. *Baltimore Sun*, November 28, 1874, 1.

8. Yale University, "Yale University Catalogue, 1820," *Yale University Catalogue* 6 (1820), accessed January 29, 2019, https://elischolar.library.yale.edu/yale_catalogue/6.

9. "Adirondack Murray's Brother Dead," *New York Sun*, January 21, 1885, 1.

10. Chauncey Murray married Martha Blackman on November 28, 1860. Martha died childless in 1874. He later married Emma Jane Bailey on January 25, 1877. Chauncey and Martha had one child, Isabella. Isabella Murray was born September 16, 1864. Chauncey died at the age of forty-seven on May 27, 1874, in his daughter's house in Englewood, New Jersey.

11. H. J. Griswold, "W. H. H. Murray by a Classmate," *New Haven Register*, June 26, 1904.

12. Joel E. Helander, *Guilford Long Ago* (Guilford, CT: 1969), 38.

13. Ruby Murray Orcutt, "Personal Impression of the Life and Work of W. H. H. (Adirondack) Murray," W. H. H. Murray Collection, MS 69-13 (Blue Mountain Lake, NY: Adirondack Museum, October 16, 1931).

14. Griswold, "W. H. H. Murray."

15. Joel Eliot Helander, *A Treasury of Guilford Places* (Guilford, CT: self-published, 2008), 80.

16. Ibid.

17. Ibid.

Chapter 2. Yale

1. Yale University, "Yale University Catalogue, 1839," *Yale University Catalogue* 25 (1839), accessed January 29, 2019; https://elischolar.library.yale.edu/yale_catalogue/25.

2. Harry Radford, *Adirondack Murray: A Biographical Appreciation*, 2nd ed. (New York: Broadway Publishing, 1906), 47.

3. Judith Schiff, "A Brief History of Yale," Yale University Library, last modified July 2, 2018; https://guides.library.yale.edu/yalehistory.

4. Yale University, "*Yale University Catalogue, 1858*," *Yale University Catalogue* 56 (1858), accessed January 29, 2019; https://elischolar.library.yale.edu/yale_catalogue/56.

5. Ibid., 24–25.

6. Ibid., 29–31.

7. Ibid., 35.

8. Ibid., 24–25.

9. W. H. H. Murray, handwritten autobiographical sketch, Murray Archives, Adirondack Experience.

10. Yale University, "Yale University Catalogue, 1835," *Yale University Catalogue* 21 (1835), accessed January 29, 2019; https://elischolar.library.yale.edu/yale_catalogue/21.

11. Yale University, "Yale University Catalogue, 1827," *Yale University Catalogue* 15 (1827), accessed January 29, 2019; https://elischolar.library.yale.edu/yale_catalogue/15.

12. Frederick G. Bascom, ed., *Letters of a Ticonderoga Farmer, Selections from the Correspondence of William H. Cook and His Wife with Their Son, Joseph Cook, 1851–1885* (Ithaca, NY: Fall Creek Books, 2010), 119, vii.

13. Ibid., x.

14. Ibid., xi.

15. Yale University, "Yale University Catalogue, 1858."

16. Bascom, *Letters of a Ticonderoga Farmer,* 49.

17. Ibid., 83.

18. Ibid., 65.

19. Ibid., 72.

20. Ibid., 82.

21. Ibid., xi.

22. Ibid., 119.

23. Charles Morris, *Famous Orators of the World and Their Best Orations* (Philadelphia: J. C. Winston Company, 1902), 311.

24. Bascom, *Letters of a Ticonderoga Farmer*, x.

25. Ibid., 83.

26. Yale University, "Yale University Catalogue, 1869" *Yale University Catalogue* 59 (1869), accessed January 29, 2019; https://elischolar.library.yale.edu/yale_catalogue/59.

27. Yale University, "Yale University Catalogue, 1872," *Yale University Catalogue* 60 (1872), accessed January 29, 2019; https://elischolar.library.yale.edu/yale_catalogue/60.

28. Yale University, "*Yale University Catalogue, 1861,*" *Yale University Catalogue* 55 (1861), accessed January 29, 2019; https://elischolar.library.yale.edu/yale_catalogue/55, and Yale University, "Yale University Catalogue, 1914," *Yale University Catalogue* 58 (1914), accessed January 29, 2019, https://elischolar.library.yale.edu/yale_catalogue/58.

29. Orcutt, "W. H. H. (Adirondack) Murray."

30. Hartford Theological Seminary, *Historical Catalogue of the Theological Institute of Connecticut* (Hartford, CT: Case Lockwood Brainard Company, 1881), 97.

Chapter 3. Seminary

1. "Mr. Murray's Stock Farm," 1.

2. "History of Hartford Seminary," Hartford Seminary, accessed January 29, 2019; https://www.hartsem.edu/about/our-history/.

3. "East Windsor Hill Historic District," Living Places, accessed January 29, 2019; http://www.livingplaces.com/CT/Hartford_County/South_Windsor_Town/East_Windsor_Hill_Historic_District.htm.

4. Daniel Sterner, *A Guide to Historic Hartford, Connecticut* (Mount Pleasant, SC: Arcadia Publishing, 2012).

5. Congregational Church, http://gene.kellerhouse-webster.com/church.html.

6. Hartford Seminary, *Historical Catalogue*, 97.

Chapter 4. Pastor

1. Radford, Adirondack Murray, 51.

2. Wilbur Stone Deming, The Church on the Green: The First Two Centuries of the First Congregational Church at Washington, Connecticut, 1741–1941 (Washington, CT: Brentano's, 1941), 135.

3. Charles Bancroft Gillespie and George Munsor Curtis, An Historic Record and Pictorial Description of the Town of Meriden (Albuquerque, NM: Journal Publishing Co., 1906), 157.

4. "History of Center Church," Center Congregational Church of Meriden, accessed January 29, 2019; https://centerchurchmeriden.files.wordpress.com/2017/03/history-of-ccc.pdf.

5. Murray, Adventures in the Wilderness, 50.

6. Margaret Lamberts Bendroth, Fundamentalists in the City: Conflict and Division in Boston's Churches, 1885–1950 (New York: Oxford University Press, 2005), 17.

7. W. H. H. Murray, Words Fitly Spoken, Selections from the Pulpit Utterances of W H H Murray, Pastor of Park Street Church (Boston: Lee and Shepard, 1873), 166.

8. Bascom, Letters of a Ticonderoga Farmer, 84.

9. "Platt, Orville Hitchcock (1827–1905)," Biographical Dictionary of the United States Congress, accessed January 29, 2019; http://bioguide.congress.gov/scripts/biodisplay.pl?index=P000382.

10. Louis A. Coolidge, An Old Fashioned Senator, Orville H. Platt, The Story of Life Unselfishly Dedicated to Public Service (New York: G. P. Putnam's Sons, The Knickerbocker Press, 1910), 13, 20.

11. Ibid., 20.

12. Ibid., 32.

13. Ibid., 54.

14. "Platt, Orville Hitchcock."

15. Coolidge, Old Fashioned Senator, 24.

16. Ibid.

17. Ibid.

18. St. Albans Daily Messenger, July 14, 1875, 3.

19. Headley, Adirondak, 143.

20. Radford, Adirondack Murray, 73.

21. Ibid.

22. Letter from Lewis & McKay, Attorneys and Counselors at Law, Rochester, New York, Dec. 22, 1903.

23. People v. Ladew, 143 N.E. 238 (NY 1924).

24. W. H. H. Murray, Mamelons and Ungava, a Legend of Saguenay (Boston: De Wolfe, Fiske, 1890), vii.

25. Ibid., viii.

Chapter 5. Park Street: 1869

1. "Population Trends in Boston 1640–1990," iBoston.org, accessed January 29, 2019; http://www.iboston.org/mcp.php?pid=popFig.

2. "National Peace Jubilee (1869)," Celebrate Boston, accessed January 29, 2019; http://www.celebrateboston.com/events/national-peace-jubilee.htm.

3. Hartley, 25.

4. "Boston University Timeline," Boston University, accessed January 29, 2019; https://www.bu.edu/timeline/.

5. "About HMS," Horace Mann School for the Deaf and Hard of Hearing, accessed January 29, 2019; https://www.bostonpublicschools.org/domain/771.

6. "About Us," Boston Children's Hospital, accessed January 29, 2019; http://www.childrenshospital.org/research/about-us/history-link.

7. "Suffragists Organize: American Woman Suffrage Association," National Women's History Museum, accessed January 29, 2019; http://www.crusadeforthe vote.org/awsa-organize/.

8. "Boston," Immigration to the United States, accessed January 29, 2019; http://immigrationtounitedstates.org/387-boston.html.

9. Ibid.

10. Murray, *Adventures in the Wilderness*, 18.

11. Park Street Church to W. H. H. Murray, October 9, 1868, Murray Archives, Adirondack Experience.

12. Elizabeth Lohnes, "Park Street Church—A History," Park Street Church, last modified October 2016; https://www.parkstreet.org/profile/history.pdf.

13. A. Z. Conrad, ed., *Commemorative Exercises at the One Hundredth Anniversary of the Organization of Park Street Church: February 26–March 3, 1909* (Boston: Park Street Centennial Committee, 1909).

14. Bendroth, *Fundamentalists in the City*, 157.

15. Conrad, *Commemorative Exercises*.

16. Bendroth, *Fundamentalists in the City*, 17.

17. H. Crosby Englizian, *Brimstone Corner: Park Street Church, Boston* (Chicago: Moody Press, 1968; Charleston, SC: BookSurge Publishing, 2009), 166. Citations refer to the BookSurge edition unless otherwise indicated.

18. Park Street Church to W. H. H. Murray.

19. Bendroth, *Fundamentalists in the City*, 159.

20. Englizian, *Brimstone Corner* (Moody ed.), 166.

21. "Ticknor & Fields," Biblio.com, accessed January 29, 2019; https://www.biblio.com/publisher/ticknor-fields.

22. "The Legacy of Publishers Ticknor and Fields at the Old Corner Bookstore," Historic Boston, last modified February 27, 2018; http://historicboston.org/the-legacy-of-publishers-ticknor-and-fields-at-the-old-corner-bookstore/.

23. Murray, *Adventures in the Wilderness*, 37–39.

24. Ibid., 39.

25. Bascom, *Letters of a Ticonderoga Farmer*, 88.

Chapter 6. Adventures in the Wilderness

1. George M. Davison, *The Fashionable Tour in 1825, An Excursion to the Springs, Niagara, Quebec and Boston* (Saratoga Springs, NY: G. M. Davison, 1825).

2. Donaldson, Alfred, L., *A History of the Adirondacks*, Harbor Hill Books, Vol. 2, 64.

3. Ibid.

4. Joel T. Headley, *The Adirondak, or Life in the Woods* (New York: Baker & Scribner, 1849).

5. Ibid., xi.

6. Ibid., 10.

7. Ibid., xii.

8. Ibid., 112.

9. Thoreau, quoted in White, *Under the Stars*, 25.

10. Murray, *Adventures in the Wilderness*, 254.

11. Headley, *Adirondak*, 167.

12. White, *Under the Stars*, 11 and 12.

13. Ibid., 5.

14. Henry David Thoreau, *Walden* (Boston: Ticknor and Fields, 1854).

15. Ibid., 104.

16. White, *Under the Stars*, 7.

17. Ibid., 25.

18. Ibid.

19. Ann Woodlief, "Ralph Waldo Emerson: 1803–1882," American Transcendentalism Web, accessed January 29, 2019; http://transcendentalism-legacy.tamu.edu/authors/emerson/.

20. "Transcendentalism, an American Philosophy," *U.S. History Online Textbook*, accessed January 29, 2019; http://www.ushistory.org/us/26f.asp.

21. Ibid.

22. White, *Under the Stars*, 14.

23. Ralph Waldo Emerson, *The Conduct of Life, Nature, and Other Essays* (J. M. Dent & Sons, 1911), 4.

24. Ralph L. Rusk, *The Letters of Ralph Waldo Emerson*, vol. 4 (New York: Columbia University Press, 1939), 365.

25. Emerson, quoted in White, *Under the Stars*, 46.

26. Ibid.

27. James Schlett, *A Not Too Greatly Changed Eden: The Story of the Philosophers' Camp in the Adirondacks* (Ithaca: Cornell University Press, 2015).

28. At the time of the encampment, the name of the pond was spelled Follansbee. Schlett, *Not Too Greatly*, 18.

29. Stillman, from Schenectady, New York, and a graduate of Union College, founded *The Crayon*, the first art magazine in the United States. He studied under Frederick Church for one year. Stillman painted *The Adirondack Club* during his time at Follensby Pond. Schlett, *Not Too Greatly*, 6, 14.

30. Oliver Wendell Holmes and Henry Wadsworth Longfellow were also invited on the trip but could not attend. Schlett, *Not Too Greatly*, 76.

31. Ibid., 58.

32. Ibid., 77.

33. "Mother J" is likely the same Mother Johnson who kept a boarding house on Raquette Falls and is mentioned in *Adventures in the Wilderness*. Ibid., 41.

34. Ibid., 80.

35. Ibid., 86.

36. Ibid., 134.

37. Young, "Murray's Rush," 13.

38. Ibid., 12.

39. "Adventures in the Wilderness," *Hartford Courant*, April 10, 1869, 1.

40. Young, "Murray's Rush," 13.

41. Murray, *Adventures in the Wilderness*, 8.

Chapter 7. The Rush

1. W. H. H. Murray, *Lake Champlain and Its Shores* (Boston: De Wolfe Fiske and Co., 1890), 38.

2. Ibid.

3. Donaldson, Alfred, L., *A History of the Adirondacks*, Vol. 1, 94.

4. Murray, *Adventures in the Wilderness*, 50.

5. Ibid.

6. "The Man Who Invented Camping," *Toronto Star*, Aug, 2, 2009.

7. Ibid.

8. Ibid.

9. Dan White, *Under the Stars: How America Fell In Love with Camping* (New York: Henry Holt, 2016), 69.

10. Frank Graham Jr., *The Adirondack Park, A Political History* (Syracuse: Syracuse University Press, 1984), 29.

11. Ibid.

12. Peggy Lynn and Sandra Weber, *Breaking Trail, Remarkable Women of the Adirondacks* (Fleischmanns, NY: Purple Mountain Press 2004), 55.

13. Ibid.

14. "The Murray Rush into the Adirondacks," *American Rifleman* 39 (1905).

15. Young, "Murray's Rush."

16. Phil Griffin, "A Short History of Saranac Lake," Bunk's Place, accessed January 29, 2019; http://www.bunksplace.com/saranac%20lake%20history.html.

17. Murray, *Adventures in the Wilderness*, 12.

18. Murray, *Lake Champlain*, 124.

19. White, *Under the Stars*, 71.

Chapter 8. Park Street

1. Radford, *Adirondack Murray*, 13.

2. Smithsonian Institution Archives, Record Unit 95, Box 28, Folder 02, Image No. SIA_000095_B28_F02_001.

3. (Utica) *Daily Observer*, Oct. 11, 1869, 1.

4. Bendroth, *Fundamentalists in the City*, 160.

5. Ibid.

6. Ibid.

7. *New York Daily Tribune*, Nov. 28, 1873.

8. Ibid.

9. W. H. H. Murray, *Music Hall Sermons*, vol. 1 (Boston: Fields, Osgood, 1870), 156.

10. Ibid., 48.

11. W. H. H. Murray, *Park Street Pulpit*, vol. 2 (Boston: James R. Osgood, 1873), 193.

12. "Rise of Industrial America, 1876–1900," Library of Congress, accessed January 29, 2019; http://www.loc.gov/teachers/classroommaterials/presentationsand activities/presentations/timeline/riseind/.

13. Barbara Goodrich, "The Protestant/Calvinistic Work Ethic," University of Colorado, Denver, accessed January 29, 2019; http://www.ucdenver.edu/facul- ty-staff/bgoodric/Pages/Protestant-Calvinist-Work-Ethic.aspx.

14. Christine Leigh Heyrman, "Puritanism and Predestination," *Divining America*, TeacherServe. National Humanities Center, accessed January 29, 2019; http://nationalhumanitiescenter.org/tserve/eighteen/ekeyinfo/puritan.htm.

15. Strauss, "Toward a Consumer Culture," 271.

16. Ibid., 274.

17. Ibid., 271.

18. Ibid.

19. Ibid., 274.

20. Kevin DeYoung, "Seven Characteristics of Liberal Theology" accessed January 29, 2019; https://www.gospelcoalition.org/blogs/kevin-deyoung/seven- characteristics-of-liberal-theology/.

21. Henry Ward Beecher, "The Nature, Importance and Liberties of Belief," in *The Original Plymouth Pulpit: Sermons of Henry Ward Beecher*, Vol. IX (1893), 291.

22. Strauss, "Toward a Consumer Culture," 277.

23. Cindy Sondik Aron, *Working at Play: A History of Vacations in the United States* (New York: Oxford University Press, 2001), 42.

24. John Noble Wilford, "How Epidemics Helped Shape the Modern Metropolis," *New York Times*, April 15, 2018.

25. White, *Under the Stars*, 61.

26. Aron, *Working at Play*, 42.

27. Strauss, "Toward a Consumer Culture," 277.

28. Ibid.

29. Donaldson, *A History of the Adirondacks*, Vol. 2, 46.

30. The Boston Daily Globe, *Boston Pulpits*, January 18, 1875, 2.

31. Strauss, "Toward a Consumer Culture."

32. W. H. H. Murray, "Living for God's Glory," in *The American Pulpit of the Day, Sermons by the Most Distinguished Living American Preachers* (London: R. D. Dickinson, 1876), 615.

33.

34. W. H. H. Murray, "The Relations of Belief to Practice," in *The American Pulpit of the Day, Sermons by the Most Distinguished Living American Preachers* (London: R. D. Dickinson, 1876), 140.

35. Murray, *Words Fitly Spoken*, at 13.

36. Strauss, "Toward a Consumer Culture," 275.

37. Ibid.

38. Ibid.

39. Murray, *Park Street Pulpit*, vol. 1, 282.

40. Murray, *Words Fitly Spoken*, at 370.

41. Strauss, "Toward a Consumer Culture," 275.

42. Bascom, *Letters of a Ticonderoga Farmer*, 90.

43. *Decatur Daily Republican*, July 14, 1874, 1.

44. W. H. H. Murray, *Prohibition vs. License*, April 28, 1867, published by his congregation and the Mass. Temperance Alliance.

45. Ibid., 8.

46. Ibid., 10.

47. Murray, *Words Fitly Spoken*, 349.

48. *The Boston Globe*, May 29, 1876, 2.

49. *The Boston Globe*, February 23, 1877, 5.

50. *The Boston Globe, Enforcement of the Prohibition Law*, October 7, 1873, 8.

51. *The Boston Daily Globe*, April 7, 1873, 8.

52. *Vermont Watchman and State Journal*, March 27, 1872, 2.

53. Marilyn E. Weigold, *The Long Island Sound: A History of its People, Places, and Environment* (New York: New York University Press, 2004), 62.

54. Frederick A. Hubbard, Greenwich CT, Nov. 24, 1917, letter to the editor, *The Sun*, Nov. 25, 1917, 8.

55. Englizian, *Brimstone Corner*, 165.

56. White, *Under the Stars*, 64.

57. A sum equal to approximately $106,000 in today's money. Park Street Church to W. H. H. Murray.

58. W. H. H. Murray, "My Record as a Lecturer," handwritten account, Murray Archives, Adirondack Experience.

59. A sum equal to between $1,500 and $4,200 in today's money. Ibid.

60. Bendroth, *Fundamentalists in the City*, 160.

61. Murray, "My Record."

62. W. H. H. Murray, *Deacons* (Boston: H. L. Shepard, 1875).

63. Ibid.

64. Ibid., 16.

Chapter 9. The Perfect Horse

1. W. H. H. Murray, *The Perfect Horse* (Boston: James R. Osgood, 1973), xi.

2. "American Incomes ca. 1650–1870," Global Price and Income History Group, accessed January 29, 2019; http://gpih.ucdavis.edu/tables.htm.

3. Helander, *Guilford Long Ago*, 38.

4. "Thoroughbred," *Britannica.com*, accessed January 29, 2019, https://www.britannica.com/animal/Thoroughbred.

5. "Thoroughbred Horse," *ScienceDaily*, accessed January 29, 2019, https://www.sciencedaily.com/terms/thoroughbred.htm.

6. Murray, *The Perfect Horse*, 126.

7. Bascom, *Letters of a Ticonderoga Farmer*, 90.

8. "Murray Stock Farm, Guildford Conn," *Spirit of the Times*, Dec. 1, 1877, 466.

9. Ida E. Hull v. Alfred G. Hull (1880), 251.

10. *Murray's Stud Farm From Grave To Gay A Remarkable Family Labor in Eastern Connecticut, Hartford Daily Courant*, Nov. 11, 1873, 4.

11. *Baltimore Sun*, Nov. 28, 1874, 1.

12. W. H. H. Murray, *The Perfect Horse* (Boston: James R. Osgood and Co., 1973).

13. Ibid.

14. Ibid., vi.

15. Ibid, 154–55.

16. *Worchester Spy*, quoted in *The American Gentlemen's Newspaper* (1873).

17. New York *Daily Graphic*, Sept 6, 1873.

18. Murray, *The Perfect Horse*, v.

19. Ibid., 302.

Chapter 10. Park Street: Separation

1. "Great Boston Fire of 1872," Boston Fire Historical Society, accessed January 29, 2019; https://bostonfirehistory.org/fires/great-boston-fire-of-1872/.

2. "Boston Fire of 1872," *Britannica.com*, accessed January 29, 2019; https://www.britannica.com/event/Boston-fire-of-1872.

3. "The Panic of 1873," *PBS.org*, accessed January 29, 2019; https://www.pbs.org/wgbh/americanexperience/features/grant-panic/.

4. Bascom, *Letters of a Ticonderoga Farmer*, 100.

5. Before the Civil War, families in America took an active role in burial of their loved ones. This changed after the war as the professionalization of the funeral process rose and family members were expected to mourn, rather than participate directly in, the death and burial process.

6. *Christian Union*, Oct. 29, 1873.

7. Englizian, *Brimstone Corner*, 172.

8. Ibid.

9. *New York World*, April 10, 1874.

10. Englizian, *Brimstone Corner*, 172.

11. Ibid., 173.

12. Park Street Church, Proceedings of Business Meetings, 1871–99, 28.

13. Englizian, *Brimstone Corner*, 173.

14. Bascom, *Letters of a Ticonderoga Farmer*, 103.

15. Englizian, *Brimstone Corner*, 173.

16. Ibid.

17. Ibid., 174.

Chapter 11. Boston Music Hall

1. Englizian, *Brimstone Corner*, 166.

2. Ed Sampson, comp., "Boston Music Hall: From Then . . . to Now," Methuen Memorial Music Hall (2015); https://mmmh.org/wp-content/uploads/2017/02/THE-BOSTON-MUSIC-HALL_-FROM-THEN-1.pdf.

3. "December 31, 1862: Boston Abolitionists Await Emancipation Proclamation," Mass Moments, accessed January 29, 2019; https://www.massmoments.org/moment-details/boston-abolitionists-await-emancipation-proclamation.html.

4. Hartley, 36.

5. "Rev. Adirondack Murray's New Church and Newspaper," *New York Herald*, Oct. 4, 1875.

6. Englizian, *Brimstone Corner*, 175.

7. Ibid., 176.

8. Murray, *Words Fitly Spoken*, 230.

9. "The Church Boston Needs," *Boston Daily Globe*, May 27, 1878, 2.

10. Englizian, *Brimstone Corner*, 176.

11. Hartley, 46–47.

12. Ibid., 48.

13. *The Boston Daily Globe*, "Boston Pulpits," Jan. 18, 1875, 2.

14. Hartley, 49.

15. Ibid., 51.

16. Ibid.

17. Ibid., 50.

18. Ibid., 27.

19. Orcutt, "W. H. H. (Adirondack) Murray."

20. Helander, *Clapboard Hill*.

21. Orcutt, "W. H. H. (Adirondack) Murray."

22. Ruby Murray Orcutt, "Personal Impressions of the Life and Works of William H. H. Murray," *The Shore Line*, 54, no. 6 (Oct. 29, 1931).

23. *The Golden Rule*, Boston, July 31, 1878.

24. Ibid.

25. *The Golden Rule*, Boston, Feb. 1879).

26. *The Golden Rule*, Boston, March 1879.

27. *The Golden Rule*, Boston, May 1879.

28. *The Golden Rule*, Boston, June 1879.

29. Hartley, 2.

30. Ibid., 4.

31. Ibid., 15.

32. Ibid., 10.

33. Ibid.

34. Bruce J. Evenson, " 'It's a Model to Many People' Dwight L. Moody, Mass Media, and the New England Revival of 1877," *The New England Quarterly* 72, no. 2 (June 1999): 251–74.

35. Hartley, 16.

36. Ibid., 25.

37. Ibid., 27.

38. Evenson, 259.

39. *The Boston Globe*, Feb. 23, 1877, 5.

40. "Popular Murrayism vs. Unpopular Spiritualism," *Spiritual Scientist* VI, no. 2, March 15, 1877, 18.

41. Ibid.

42. Ibid.

43. *St. Albans Daily Messenger*, June 10, 1873, 2.

44. Karen DePauw, "Scandal in the Beecher Family," Connecticut History.org, accessed January 29, 2019; https://connecticuthistory.org/scandal-in-the-beecher-family/.

45. "Mabel Irwin," Ancestry.com, accessed January 29, 2019; https://www.ancestry.com/search/categories/bmd_death/?name=Mabel_Irwin&birth=1856&death=1928.

46. "Mr. Murray in California," *New York Sun*, Aug. 5, 1879.

47. "What Miss Hodgkins Says," *New York Sun*, Aug. 6, 1879.

48. Ibid.

49. Abbott C. Page, "Life of W. H. H. Murray, as Remembered by Friends Who Knew Him Well," *Shore Line Rimes*, Nov. 24, 1932.

50. Griswold, "W. H. H. Murray."

51. Ibid.

52. *The Golden Rule*, Boston, June 1879.

53. "A Microcosmic History of the Carriage Industry of the United States. A Few Leading Carriage Centers," *Hub* (Oct. 1897): 420–30.

54. "Adirondack Murray, An Interview with the Celebrated Preacher," *Chicago Tribune*, Aug. 28, 1879, 12.

55. "Where Is Parson Murray?" *The Sun*, New York, Aug. 2, 1879.

56. "A Microcosmic History," 420–30.

57. *New York Evening Post*, April 17, 1879.

58. *Gazette and Courier*, Greenfield, MA, Sept. 8, 1879.

59. "A Microcosmic History," 420–30.

60. Radford, *Adirondack Murray*, 69.

61. Murray, *Adventures in the Wilderness*, 26.

62. *Democratic Advocate*, Nov. 2, 1878, 2.

63. *Lowell Daily Courier.*

64. "Adirondack Murray's Affairs," *New York World*, Aug. 5, 1879.

65. "Rev. W. H. H. Murray's Embarrassments," *Lowell Daily Carrier*, Aug. 5, 1879.

66. "The Reverend W. H. H. Murray," *The Sun*, Sept. 6, 1874, 1.

67. *Harris County Journal*, 1879.

68. "A Plump Denial," *Boston Weekly Globe*, Sept. 9, 1879.

69. Ibid.

70. Ibid.

71. "The Panic of 1873," The History Engine, accessed January 29, 2019. https://historyengine.richmond.edu/episodes/view/308.

72. "Industrial Capitalism."

73. Martin Armstrong, "The Long Depression—The First Great Depression," last modified July 16, 2015; https://www.armstrongeconomics.com/history/americas-economic-history/the-long-depression-the-first-great-depression/.

74. "The Amassing of Wealth, Mr. Murray Lectures on 'How to Become a Millionaire,'" *Clinton Eye*, Clinton, MO, Jan. 19, 1889.

75. Murray, *Adventures in the Wilderness*, 28.

76. *New York Evening Post*, Nov. 10, 1925.

77. Ibid.

78. Isadora L. Murray to W. H. H. Murray, Dec. 10, 1884, Murray Archives, Adirondack Experience.

79. "Adirondack Murray's Wife Wants a Divorce," *Evening Star*, Washington, DC, Oct. 1, 1885, 1.

80. *Willoughby Independent*, June 6, 1884.

81. *New York Daily Tribune*, March 11, 1884.

82. *New York Evening Post*, Nov. 10, 1925.

83. *Essex County Republican*, June 1, 1882.

84. "Rev. Mabel McCoy Hodgkins Irwin," Find a Grave, accessed January 29, 2019; https://www.findagrave.com/cemetery/online/68437175.

85. "Woman Preacher," *The Boston Globe*, March 14, 1895, 1.

86. "Rev. Mabel McCoy of Mansfield," *Boston Daily Advertiser*, May 10, 1895, 5.

87. "Mrs. McCoy Not the First," *The Boston Globe*, March 25, 1895, 6.

Chapter 12. Texas

1. W. H. H. Murray, handwritten advertisement for lecture series, Murray Archives, Adirondack Experience.

2. Radford, *Adirondack Murray*, 75.

3. "Murray's Queer Conduct," *Oswego Palladium* (1879).

4. Ibid.

5. Reprinted in "Murray's Queer Conduct."

6. *Brooklyn Daily Eagle*, Aug. 25, 1879.

7. "Parson Murray, He Talks Freely to a 'Frisco Reporter," *Boston Weekly Globe*, Sept. 2, 1879.

8. Reprinted in "Murray's Queer Conduct."

9. "Goodbye Murray," *New York Evening Telegram*, Sept. 8, 1879.

10. Murray, *Adventures in the Wilderness*, 28.

11. Alwyn Barr, "Late Nineteenth Century Texas," *Handbook of Texas Online*, accessed January 29, 2019; https://tshaonline.org/handbook/online/articles/np l01.

12. Ibid.

13. Laurie E. Jasinski, "San Antonio, TX," *Handbook of Texas Online*, accessed January 29, 2019; https://tshaonline.org/handbook/online/articles/hds02.

14. *Chicago Tribune*, March 20, 1883, 4.

15. Reprinted in *Wallace's Monthly* 9, no. 1 (Feb. 1883): 271.

16. "Murray Explains," *Daily Sentinel*, Rome, NY, April 6, 1883.

17. Ibid.

18. Ibid.

19. "The Murray Muddle," *The San Francisco Examiner*, April 7, 1883, 8.

20. Ibid.

21. Ibid.

22. Ibid.

Chapter 13. Montreal

1. Dany Fougères, Roderick MacLeo, *Montreal: The History of a North American City* (Montreal: McGill-Queen's Press, 2018), 357.

2. Paul-André Linteau, "Montreal," *The Canadian Encyclopedia*, last modified November 9, 2017; https://www.thecanadianencyclopedia.ca/en/article/montreal/.

3. Ibid.

4. "Adirondack Murray. He Runs a Café and Causes a Little Sensation in Montreal," *Rochester Democrat and Chronicle*, Dec. 26, 1884.

5. *Albany Express*, July 18, 1885.

6. *New York World*, Dec. 31, 1884.

7. "Murray's Café," *Kansas City Times*, Dec. 29, 1884, 8.

8. Ibid.

9. "Small Pox in Montreal," *The Boston Daily Globe*, Nov. 3, 1885, 6.

10. John Kalbfleisch, "From the Archives: Buffalo Bill, Sitting Bull Brought West to Montreal," *Montreal Gazette*, Aug. 16, 1996, last modified August 15, 2017; https://montrealgazette.com/sponsored/mtl-375th/from-the-archives-buffalo-bill-sitting-bull-brought-west-to-montreal.

11. Vicky Lapointe, "Buffalo Bill et le Wild West Show [août 1885, Montréal]," Patrimoine, Histoire et Multimédia, March 3, 2012; https://tolkien2008.wordpress.com/2012/03/03/buffalo-bill-et-le-wild-west-show-aout-1885-montreal/.

12. Ibid.

13. Ibid.

14. Photograph by William Notman, Montreal 1885.

15. Deanne Stillman, "The Unlikely Alliance Between Buffalo Bill and Sitting Bull," *History.com*, accessed January 29, 2019; https://www.history.com/news/the-unlikely-alliance-between-buffalo-bill-and-sitting-bull.

16. James McLaughlin, "An Account of Sitting Bull's Death" (Philadelphia, 1891), *PBS.org*, accessed January 29, 2019; https://www.pbs.org/weta/thewest/resources/archives/eight/sbarrest.htm.

17. "The Dead Sioux Chief. Adirondack Murray Pays a Tribute to Sitting Bull," *New York World*, Dec. 21, 1890.

18. Ibid.

Chapter 14. Burlington

1. *Argus and Patriot*, November 11, 1885, 2.

2. 1920 United States Federal Census, Connecticut, New Haven, Guilford, District 0260.

3. Nathan Clark to Frances Rivers, Murray Archives, Adirondack Experience.

4. Ibid.

5. Nathan Clark to Frances Rivers, April 5, 1886, Murray Archives, Adirondack Experience.

6. Ibid.

7. All may not be as it seems when it comes to the Clarke missives. A careful comparison of the handwriting of Clarke and that of Fannie Bursley reveals

an astonishing similarity. It is possible that the author of the Clarke letters was actually Bursley, seeking to scare Rivers away from Murray and the home and life she shared with the man she loved.

8. "Adirondack Murray Married in Burlington Vt., to a Montreal Lady," *Burlington Weekly Free Press*, Oct. 14, 1886.

9. "Adirondack Murray Married in Burlington, Vt, to a Montreal Lady," *Burlington Free Press*, Oct. 15, 1886.

10. *Burlington City Directory 1888–89* (Burlington, VT: L. P. Waite).

11. *Burlington City Directory 1889–90* (Burlington, VT: L. P. Waite).

12. Murray, *Daylight Land*.

13. *Burlington City Directory 1889–90*.

14. Marguerita Murray to W. H. H. Murray, Murray Archives, Adirondack Experience.

15. Marguerita Murray to W. H. H. Murray, August 1886, Murray Archives, Adirondack Experience.

16. A. M. Locke to W. H. H. Murray March 18, 1887, Murray Archives, Adirondack Experience.

17. Ibid.

18. Deed of burial lot dated August 16, 1886, Lake View Cemetery.

19. "Annie M. F. Murray," Find a Grave, accessed January 29, 2019; https://www.findagrave.com/memorial/155588710/annie-m._f.-murray.

20. Jone Johnson Lewis, "Free Love," Thought Co., last modified July 31, 2017; https://www.thoughtco.com/free-love-and-womens-history-3530392.

21. Kathleen Hulser, "Free Love, Emma Goldman and Victoria Woodhull," New York History Blog, last modified February 20, 2013; https://newyorkhistory-blog.org/2013/02/20/free-love-emma-goldman-and-victoria-woodhull/.

22. Lewis, "Free Love."

23. Hal Sears, *The Sex Radicals: Free Love in High Victorian America* (Lawrence: University Press of Kansas, 1977), 4–5.

24. *Orleans Republican*, Albion, New York, October 17, 1883.

25. Ibid.

26. *New York Herald*, Oct. 8, 1883.

27. Ibid.

28. Ibid.

29. Ibid.

30. Ibid.

31. "He spoke to me, for the first time in his life, of intemperance as one of the public evils he resisted from an agonizing personal experience in regard to his own father, who does not now live with his mother and is intemperate." Bascom, *Letters of a Ticonderoga Farmer*, 90.

32. W. H. H. Murray, "A Handbook on Marriage and Divorce," unpublished manuscript, Murray Archives, Adirondack Experience.

33. Ibid.

34. Ibid., 7.

35. Ibid., 9.

36. Ibid., 20.

37. Ibid.

38. Ibid., 23.

39. Ibid., 30.

40. Ibid., 31.

41. Ibid., 37.

42. Wendy McElroy, "The Free Love Movement and Radical Individualism in the 19th Century," *Libertarian Enterprise* no. 15 (October 1, 1996); http://www.ncc-1776.org/tle1996/le961008.html.

Chapter 15. Burlington

1. "The White Wings on Lake Champlain," *Troy Daily Times*, March 23, 1887.

2. "LCYC Chronology—1886–1998," Lake Champlain Yacht Club, accessed January 29, 2019; https://lcyc.info/club/history/chronology.

3. "Lake Champlain Yacht Club," *Outing* 13 (October 1888–March 1889): 343.

4. Howard I. Chapelle, *The Migrations of an American Boat Type*, EBook, Project Gutenberg, 2009; https//www.gutenberg.org/files/29285/29285-h/29285-h.htm.

5. *The Burlington Free Press*, Aug. 11, 1886, 5.

6. *Outing,* 18, no. 2 (May 1891): 97.

7. *Constitution and By-Laws of the Lake Champlain Yacht Club, Burlington, Vermont, With the Sailing Regulations, Officers, Membership and Yachts* (Burlington: Free Press, 1892), 20.

8. *Outing,* no. 2 (May 1891): 103.

9. Ibid.

10. Ibid.

11. "LCYC Chronology."

12. "Lake Champlain Yacht Club," 340.

13. "LCYC Chronology."

14. "The History of Champ the Lake Monster," Lake Champlain Region, accessed January 29, 2019; http://www.lakechamplainregion.com/heritage/champ.

15. *New York Times*, May 22, 1887.

16. Ibid.

17. Ibid.

18. W. H. H. Murray, *Daylight Land* (Boston: Cupples and Hurd, 1888).

19. Murray, *Mamelons and Ungava*, x.

20. Ibid.

21. W. H. H. Murray, *The Doom of Mamelons* (Philadelphia: Hubbard Brothers, 1888).

22. Murray, *Lake Champlain.*

23. Ibid., 45.

24. Ibid., 58.

25. Ibid., 188.

26. Ibid., 115.

27. Ibid., 124.

28. Ibid., 139.

29. Ibid.

30. Ibid., 140.

31. Ibid., 162.

32. Joel E. Helander, *Clapboard Hill Newspaper*, Feb. 1968.

Chapter 16. Home and Family

1. W. H. H. Murray, "Our National Policy. Shall it be Continental of Imperialistic?" Connecticut River Valley Chautauqua at Laurel Park, July 20, 1898.

2. W. H. H. Murray letter to family, November 12, 1890, Murray Archives, Adirondack Experience.

3. W. H. H. Murray, *How I Am Educating My Daughters; Or, A Practical Illustration of What Can Easily Be Done in Development of Their Loved Ones by Parents at Home*, 2nd ed. (Hartford: Case, Lockwood and Brainard, 1902).

Chapter 17. How I Am Educating My Daughters

1. Murray, *How I am Educating*, 151.

2. Ibid., 8.

3. Ibid., 23.

4. Murray, *Words Fitly Spoken*, 375.

5. Ibid., 260.

6. William J. Reese, "The Origins of Progressive Education," *History of Education Quarterly* 41, no. 1 (Spring 2001): 7.

7. Ibid., 9.

8. Ibid., 3.

9. Ibid., 20.

10. Ibid., 2.

11. Ibid., 25.

12. Ibid., cover page.

13. Ibid., 44.

14. Ibid., 191.

15. Ibid., 30.

16. Ibid., 29.

17. Ibid., 35.

18. Griswold, "W. H. H. Murray."

19. Murray, *How I Am Educating*.

20. "His Grave under an Apple Tree. There Adirondack Murray Will Be Buried It Stands on the Lawn of His Guilford Home The Clergyman, Author, Stockbreeder, and Lecturer Dies after an Illness of Less Than a Week—Devoted to His Children and His Home," *The Hartford Courant*, March 4, 1904, 9.

21. Helander, *Clapboard Hill*.

22. Orcutt, "W. H. H. (Adirondack) Murray."

23. Later renamed Roosevelt Island. "What Was Blackwell's Island," New-York Historical Society Museum & Library, accessed January 29, 2019; https://www.nyhistory.org/community/blackwells-island.

24. "Blackwell's Island Chaplain Awarded Divorce Here Today," *Bridgeport Times & Evening Farmer*, May 16, 1919, 1.

25. *Journal of the Proceedings of the National Education Association* 50 (1912).

26. "Ruby Rivers Murray 1912," A Postcard Collection of Mount Holyoke College, accessed January 29, 2019; https://www.mtholyoke.edu/~dalbino//letters/women/rmurray.html. Also *Cornell Chemist* 9–11 (1919): 32.

27. "Ruby Rivers Murray 1912."

28. "Ruby Rivers Murray," Ginaology, accessed January 29, 2019, http://www.ginaology.com/rootspersona-tree/ruby-rivers-murray/.

29. "Ruby Rivers Murray 1912."

30. Connecticut Death Index, 1949–2012.

31. "Grace Norton (Murray) Williamson," Goodwin-Genealogy Wikia, accessed January 29, 2019; http://goodwingenealogy.wikia.com/wiki/Grace_Norton_(Murray)_Williamson.

32. "Theatre Recruiting Fills Depleted Ranks of the 4th Company," *The Farmer*, May 25, 2017.

33. *Hartford Daily Courant*, March 3, 1921.

34. "Grace Norton."

35. "Organizer of Women Given Appointment," *Bridgeport Telegram*, Oct. 25, 1923.

36. Episcopal Diocese of New York, New York.

37. "Grace Norton."

38. Episcopal Diocese of New York.

39. "The Passing Show of 1917," Playbill, accessed January 29, 2019; http://www.playbill.com/production/the-passing-show-of-1917-winter-garden-theatre-vault-0000011649.

40. Frances Rivers Murray to Ethel Murray, Murray Archives, Adirondack Experience.

41. "Alienation Suit for $350,000 by Mrs. Thomas Beach," *Hartford Times*, Nov. 16, 1923.

42. Ibid.

43. "Milton Tenney MacDonald," Ginaology, accessed January 29, 2019; http://www.ginaology.com/rootspersona-tree/milton-tenney-macdonald/.

44. State of Massachusetts, *Massachusetts Death Index, 1970–2003* (Boston: Commonwealth of Massachusetts Department of Health Services, 2005).

45. "Milton Tenney MacDonald."

46. *1920 United States Federal Census* (database online) (Provo, UT: Ancestry. com Operations, 2010).

47. "Connecticut Deaths and Burials, 1772–1934" (index) (Salt Lake City, FamilySearch, 2009, 2010). Index entries are derived from digital copies of original and compiled records.

Bibliography

About HMS. Horace Mann School for the Deaf and Hard of Hearing. Accessed January 29, 2019; https://www.bostonpublicschools.org/domain/771.

About Us. Boston Children's Hospital. Accessed January 29, 2019; http://www.childrenshospital.org/research/about-us/history-link.

"Adirondack Murray, An Interview with the Celebrated Preacher." *Chicago Tribune*, August 28, 1879.

"Adirondack Murray. He Runs a Café and Causes a Little Sensation in Montreal." *Rochester Democrat and Chronicle*, December 26, 1884.

"Adirondack Murray Married in Burlington VT., to a Montreal Lady." *Burlington Weekly Free Press*, October 14, 1886.

"Adirondack Murray's Affairs." *New York World*, August 5, 1879.

"Adirondack Murray's Brother Dead." *New York Sun*, January 21, 1885.

"Adirondack Murray's Wife Wants a Divorce." Washington *Evening Star*, October 1, 1885.

"Adventures in the Wilderness." *Hartford Courant*, April 10, 1869.

"Alienation Suit for $350,000 by Mrs. Thomas Beach." *Hartford Times*, November 16, 1923.

American Incomes ca. 1650–1870. Global Price and Income History Group. Accessed January 29, 2019; http://gpih.ucdavis.edu/tables.htm.

"The Amassing of Wealth, Mr. Murray Lectures on 'How to Become a Millionaire.'" *Clinton* (MO) *Eye*, January 19, 1889.

Armstrong, Martin. "The Long Depression—The First Great Depression." Last modified July 16, 2015; https://www.armstrongeconomics.com/history/americas-economic-history/the-long-depression-the-first-great-depression.

Aron, Cindy Sondik. *Working at Play: A History of Vacations in the United States*. New York: Oxford University Press, 2001.

Barr, Alwyn. "Late Nineteenth Century Texas." *Handbook of Texas Online*. Accessed January 29, 2019; https://tshaonline.org/handbook/online/articles/npl01.

Bascom, Frederick G., ed. *Letters of a Ticonderoga Farmer, Selections from the Correspondence of William H. Cook and His Wife with Their Son, Joseph Cook, 1851–1885*. Ithaca, NY: Fall Creek Books, 2010.

Beecher, Henry Ward. "The Nature, Importance and Liberties of Belief." In *The Original Plymouth Pulpit: Sermons of Henry Ward Beecher*, Vol. IX (1893).

Bendroth, Margaret Lamberts. *Fundamentalists in the City: Conflict and Division in Boston's Churches, 1885–1950*. New York: Oxford University Press, 2005.

"Blackwell's Island Chaplain Awarded Divorce Here Today." *Bridgeport Times & Evening Farmer*, May 16, 1919.

Boston Fire of 1872. Britannica.com. Accessed January 29, 2019; https://www.britannica.com/event/Boston-fire-of-1872.

"Boston Pulpits." *The Boston Daily Globe*, January 18, 1875.

Boston University Timeline. Boston University. Accessed January 29, 2019; https://www.bu.edu/timeline/.

Boston, Immigration to the United States. Accessed January 29, 2019; http://immigrationtounitedstates.org/387-boston.html.

Burlington City Directory 1888–89. Burlington, VT: L. P. Waite.

Burlington City Directory 1889–90. Burlington, VT: L. P. Waite.

Chapelle, Howard I. *The Migrations of an American Boat Type*. EBook. Project Gutenberg, 2009.

"The Church Boston Needs." *Boston Daily Globe*, May 27, 1878.

Conrad, A. Z., ed. *Commemorative Exercises at the One Hundredth Anniversary of the Organization of Park Street Church: February 26–March 3, 1909*. Boston: Park Street Centennial Committee, 1909.

Constitution and By-Laws of the Lake Champlain Yacht Club, Burlington, Vermont, With the Sailing Regulations, Officers, Membership, and Yachts. Burlington: Free Press, 1892.

Coolidge, Louis A. *An Old Fashioned Senator, Orville H. Platt, The Story of Life Unselfishly Dedicated to Public Service*. New York: G. P. Putnam's Sons, The Knickerbocker Press, 1910.

Davison, George M. *The Fashionable Tour in 1825, An Excursion to the Springs, Niagara, Quebec, and Boston*. Saratoga Springs: G. M. Davison, 1825.

"The Dead Sioux Chief. Adirondack Murray Pays a Tribute to Sitting Bull." *New York World*, December 21, 1890.

December 31, 1862: Boston Abolitionists Await Emancipation Proclamation. Mass Moments. Accessed January 29, 2019; https://www.massmoments.org/moment-details/boston-abolitionists-await-emancipation-proclamation.html.

Deming, Wilbur Stone. *The Church on the Green: The First Two Centuries of the First Congregational Church at Washington, Connecticut, 1741–1941*. Washington, CT: Brentano's, 1941.

DePauw, Karen "Scandal in the Beecher Family," ConnecticutHistory.org. Accessed January 29, 2019; https://connecticuthistory.org/scandal-in-the-beecher-family/.

DeYoung, Kevin, "Seven Characteristics of Liberal Theology." Accessed January 29, 2019; https://www.gospelcoalition.org/blogs/kevin-deyoung/seven-characteristics-of-liberal-theology/.

Donaldson, Alfred L. *A History of the Adirondacks*, Vol. 1. Harbor Hill Books.

————. *A History of the Adirondacks,* Vol. 2. Harbor Hill Books.

East Windsor Hill Historic District. Living Places. Accessed January 29, 2019; http://www.livingplaces.com/CT/Hartford_County/South_Windsor_Town/East_Windsor_Hill_Historic_District.htm.

Emerson, Ralph Waldo. *The Conduct of Life, Nature, and Other Essays.* J. M. Dent and Sons, 1911.

"Enforcement of the Prohibition Law." *The Boston Globe,* October 7, 1873.

Englizian, H. Crosby. *Brimstone Corner: Park Street Church, Boston.* Chicago: Moody Press, 1968; Charleston, SC: BookSurge, 2009.

Fougères, Dany Roderick MacLeo. *Montreal: The History of a North American City.* Montreal: McGill-Queen's Press, 2018.

The Golden Rule. Boston. July 31, 1878.

The Golden Rule. Boston. February 1879.

The Golden Rule. Boston. March 1879.

The Golden Rule. Boston May 1879.

The Golden Rule. Boston. June 1879.

Goodrich, Barbara, "The Protestant/Calvinistic Work Ethic." University of Colorado, Denver. Accessed January 29, 2019; http://www.ucdenver.edu/faculty-staff/bgoodric/Pages/Protestant-Calvinist-Work-Ethic.aspx.

"Goodbye Murray." *New York Evening Telegram,* September 8, 1879.

Gillespie, Charles Bancroft, and George Munsor Curtis. *An Historic Record and Pictorial Description of the Town of Meriden.* Albuquerque, NM: Journal Publishing Co., 1906.

Grahm Jr., Frank. *The Adirondack Park, A Political History.* Syracuse: Syracuse University Press, 1984.

Great Boston Fire of 1872. Boston Fire Historical Society. Accessed January 29, 2019; https://bostonfirehistory.org/fires/great-boston-fire-of-1872/.

Griffin, Phil. "A Short History of Saranac Lake." Bunk's Place. Accessed January 29, 2019; http://www.bunksplace.com/saranac%20lake%20history.html.

Griswold, H. J. "W.H.H. Murray by a Classmate." *New Haven Register,* June 26, 1904.

Hartford Theological Seminary. *Historical Catalogue of the Theological Institute of Connecticut.* Hartford: Case Lockwood Brainard, 1881.

Headley, Joel T. *The Adirondak, or Life in the Woods.* New York: Baker and Scribner, 1849.

Helander, Joel E. *Guilford Long Ago.* Self-published. Guilford, CT, 1969.

————. *A Treasury of Guilford Places.* Self-published. Guilford, CT, 2008.

Heyrman, Christine Leigh. "Puritanism and Predestination." *Divining America.* TeacherServe, National Humanities Center. Accessed January 29, 2019; http://nationalhumanitiescenter.org/tserve/eighteen/ekeyinfo/puritan.htm.

History of Center Church. Center Congregational Church of Meriden. Accessed January 29, 2019; https://centerchurchmeriden.files.wordpress.com/2017/03/history-of-ccc.pdf.

History of Hartford Seminary. Hartford Seminary; Accessed January 29, 2019; https://www.hartsem.edu/about/our-history/.

The History of Champ the Lake Monster. Lake Champlain Region. Accessed January 29, 2019; http://www.lakechamplainregion.com/heritage/champ.

"The Legacy of Publishers Ticknor and Fields at the Old Corner Bookstore." Historic Boston. Last modified February 27, 2018; http://historicboston. org/the-legacy-of-publishers-ticknor-and-fields-at-the-old-corner-bookstore/.

Historical Overview, Town of Guilford. Accessed January 29, 2019; http://www. ci.guilford.ct.us/about-guilford/historical-overview/.

Hulser, Kathleen. "Free Love, Emma Goldman and Victoria Woodhull." New York History Blog. Last modified February 20, 2013; https://newyorkhistoryblog. org/2013/02/20/free-love-emma-goldman-and-victoria-woodhull/.

Jasinski, Laurie E. "San Antonio, TX." *Handbook of Texas* Online. Accessed January 29, 2019; https://tshaonline.org/handbook/online/articles/hds02.

Journal of the Proceedings of the National Education Association 50 (1912).

Kalbfleisch, John. "From the Archives: Buffalo Bill, Sitting Bull Brought West to Montreal." *Montreal Gazette*, August 16, 1996. Last modified August 15, 2017; https://montrealgazette.com/sponsored/mtl-375th/from-the-archives-buffalo-bill-sitting-bull-brought-west-to-montreal.

Lapointe, Vicky. "Buffalo Bill et le Wild West Show [août 1885, Montréal]." Patrimoine, Histoire et Multimédia. March 3, 2012; https://tolkien2008.wordpress. com/2012/03/03/buffalo-bill-et-le-wild-west-show-aout-1885-montreal/.

Lake Champlain Yacht Club. *Outing* 13 (October 1888–March 1889).

"LCYC Chronology—1886–1998." Lake Champlain Yacht Club. Accessed January 29, 2019; https://lcyc.info/club/history/chronology.

Lewis, Jone Johnson. "Free Love." Thought Co. Last modified July 31, 2017; https:// www.thoughtco.com/free-love-and-womens-history-3530392.

Linteau, Paul-André. "Montreal." *The Canadian Encyclopedia.* Last modified November 9, 2017; https://www.thecanadianencyclopedia.ca/en/article/montreal/.

Lohnes, Elizabeth. "Park Street Church—A History." Park Street Church. Last modified October 2016; https://www.parkstreet.org/profile/history.pdf.

Lynn, Peggy, and Sandra Weber. *Breaking Trail, Remarkable Women of the Adirondacks.* Fleischmanns, NY: Purple Mountain Press 2004.

"The Man Who Invented Camping." *Toronto Star*, August 2, 2009.

McElroy, Wendy. "The Free Love Movement and Radical Individualism in the 19th Century." *Libertarian Enterprise* no. 15 (October 1, 1996); http://www. ncc-1776.org/tle1996/le961008.html.

McLaughlin, James. "An Account of Sitting Bull's Death," (Philadelphia, 1891). *PBS.org.* Accessed January 29, 2019; https://www.pbs.org/weta/thewest/ resources/archives/eight/sbarrest.htm.

"A Microcosmic History of the Carriage Industry of the United States: A Few Leading Carriage Centers." *Hub*, October 1897.

Morris, Charles. *Famous Orators of the World and Their Best Orations*. Philadelphia: J. C. Winston, 1902.

"Mr. Murray's Stock Farm." *New York Sun*, August 6, 1879.

"Mr. Murray's Farm." *Baltimore Sun*, November 28, 1874.

"Mr. Murray in California." *New York Sun*, August 5, 1879.

"Mrs. McCoy Not the First." *The Boston Globe*, March 25, 1895.

"Murray Explains." *Daily Sentinel* (Rome, NY), April 6, 1883.

"The Murray Muddle." *The San Francesco Examiner*, April 7, 1883.

"The Murray Rush into the Adirondacks." *American Rifleman* 39 (1905).

"Murray Stock Farm, Guildford Conn." *Spirit of the Times*, December 1, 1877.

"Murray's Café." *Kansas City Times*, December 29, 1884.

"Murray's Queer Conduct." *Oswego Palladium*, 1879.

Murray, W. H. H. "A Handbook on Marriage and Divorce." Unpublished manuscript. Murray Archives, Adirondack Experience.

———. *Adventures in the Wilderness*. Syracuse: Adirondack Museum, 1970.

———. *Daylight Land*. Boston: Cupples and Hurd, 1888.

———. *Deacons*. Boston: H. L. Shepard, 1875.

———. *The Doom of Mamelons*. Philadelphia: Hubbard Brothers, 1888.

———. *Holiday Tales, Christmas in the Adirondacks*. Springfield, MA: Springfield Printing and Binding, 1897.

———. *How I Am Educating My Daughters; Or, A Practical Illustration of What Can Easily Be Done in Development of Their Loved Ones by Parents at Home*, 2nd ed. Hartford: Case, Lockwood and Brainard, 1902.

———. *Lake Champlain and Its Shores*. Boston: De Wolfe Fiske, 1890.

———. "Living for God's Glory." In *The American Pulpit of the Day, Sermons by the Most Distinguished Living American Preachers*. London: R. D. Dickinson, 1876.

———. *Mamelons and Ungava, a Legend of Saguenay*. Boston: De Wolfe, Fiske, 1890.

———. *Music Hall Sermons*, vol. 1. Boston: Fields, Osgood, 1870.

———. "Our National Policy. Shall it be Continental of Imperialistic?" Connecticut River Valley Chautauqua at Laurel Park, July 20, 1898.

———. *Park Street* Pulpit, vol. 2. Boston: James R. Osgood, 1873.

———. *The Perfect Horse*. Boston: James R. Osgood, 1873.

———. *Prohibition vs. License*. Published by his congregation and the Mass. Temperance Alliance, April 28, 1867.

———. "The Relations of Belief to Practice." In *The American Pulpit of the Day, Sermons by the Most Distinguished Living American Preachers*. London: R. D. Dickinson, 1876.

———. *Words Fitly Spoken, Selections from the Pulpit Utterances of W H Murray, Pastor of Park Street Church*. Boston: Lee and Shepard, 1873.

National Peace Jubilee (1869). Celebrate Boston. Accessed January 29, 2019; http://www.celebrateboston.com/events/national-peace-jubilee.htm.

Nietering, Kristen, Jordan Sorensen, and Mary Dunne. *A Short History of Guilford from Historic and Architectural Resources Inventory for the Town of Guilford, Connecticut Phase II Supplemental Survey.* Hartford: State of Connecticut, 2015.

Orcutt, Ruby Murray. "Personal Impressions of the Life and Works of William H. H. Murray." *The Shore Line* 54, no. 6 (October 29, 1931).

"Organizer of Women Given Appointment." *Bridgeport Telegram*, October 25, 1923.

Page, Abbott C. "Life of W. H. H. Murray, as Remembered by Friends Who Knew Him Well." *Shore Line Rimes*, November 24, 1932.

The Panic of 1873. PBS.org. Accessed January 29, 2019; https://www.pbs.org/wgbh/americanexperience/features/grant-panic/.

Park Street Church, Proceedings of Business Meetings, 1871–99.

"Parson Murray, He Talks Freely to a 'Frisco Reporter." *Boston Weekly Globe*, September 2, 1879.

The Passing Show of 1917. Playbill. Accessed January 29, 2019; http://www.playbill.com/production/the-passing-show-of-1917-winter-garden-theatre-vault-0000011649.

"A Plump Denial." *Boston Weekly Globe*, September 9, 1879.

"Popular Murrayism v. Unpopular Spiritualism." *Spiritual Scientist* VI., no. 2 (March 15, 1877).

Population Trends in Boston 1640–1990. iBoston.org. Accessed January 29, 2019; http://www.iboston.org/mcp.php?pid=popFig.

"Platt, Orville Hitchcock (1827–1905)." *Biographical Dictionary of the United States Congress.* Accessed January 29, 2019; http://bioguide.congress.gov/scripts/biodisplay.pl?index=P000382.

Radford, Harry. *Adirondack Murray: A Biographical Appreciation*, 2nd ed. New York: Broadway Publishing, 1906.

Reese, William J. "The Origins of Progressive Education." *History of Education Quarterly* 41, no. 1 (Spring 2001).

"Rev. Adirondack Murray's New Church and Newspaper." *New York Herald*, October 4, 1875.

"Rev. Mabel McCoy of Mansfield." *Boston Daily Advertiser*, May 10, 1895.

"The Reverend W. H. H. Murray." *The Sun*, September 6, 1874.

"Rev. W. H. H. Murray Is in Trouble." *North Star* (Danville, VT), August 8, 1879.

"Rev. W. H. H. Murray's Embarrassments," *Lowell Daily Carrier*, August 5, 1879.

Rise of Industrial America, 1876–1900. Library of Congress. Accessed January 29, 2019; http://www.loc.gov/teachers/classroommaterials/presentationsand activities/presentations/timeline/riseind/.

Ruby Rivers Murray 1912. A Postcard Collection of Mount Holyoke College. Accessed January 29, 2019; https://www.mtholyoke.edu/~dalbino//letters/women/rmurray.html. Also: *Cornell Chemist* 9–11 (1919).

Rusk, Ralph L. *The Letters of Ralph Waldo Emerson,* vol. 4. New York: Columbia University Press, 1939.

Sampson, Ed, comp. "Boston Music Hall: From Then . . . to Now," Methuen Memorial Music Hall (2015); https://mmmh.org/wp-content/uploads/2017/02/THE-BOSTON-MUSIC-HALL_-FROM-THEN-1.pdf.

Schiff, Judith. *A Brief History of Yale.* Yale University Library. Last modified July 2, 2018; https://guides.library.yale.edu/yalehistory.

Schlett, James. *A Not Too Greatly Changed Eden: The Story of the Philosophers' Camp in the Adirondacks.* Ithaca: Cornell University Press, 2015.

Sears, Hal. *The Sex Radicals: Free Love in High Victorian America.* Lawrence: University Press of Kansas, 1977.

Sterner, Daniel. *A Guide to Historic Hartford, Connecticut.* Mount Pleasant, SC: Arcadia, 2012.

Stillman, Deanne "The Unlikely Alliance Between Buffalo Bill and Sitting Bull." History.com. Accessed January 29, 2019; https://www.history.com/news/the-unlikely-alliance-between-buffalo-bill-and-sitting-bull.

Suffragists Organize: American Woman Suffrage Association. National Women's History Museum. Accessed January 29, 2019; http://www.crusadeforthevote.org/awsa-organize/.

"Theatre Recruiting Fills Depleted Ranks of the 4th Company" *The Farmer,* May 25, 2017.

Thoreau, Henry David. *Walden.* Boston: Ticknor and Fields, 1854.

Thoroughbred. Britannica.com. Accessed January 29, 2019; https://www.britannica.com/animal/Thoroughbred.

Thoroughbred Horse. ScienceDaily. Accessed January 29, 2019; https://www.sciencedaily.com/terms/thoroughbred.htm.

Ticknor and Fields. Biblio.com. Accessed January 29, 2019; https://www.biblio.com/publisher/ticknor-fields.

Transcendentalism, an American Philosophy. U.S. History Online Textbook. Accessed January 29, 2019; http://www.ushistory.org/us/26f.asp.

Weigold, Marilyn E. *The Long Island Sound: A History of its People, Places and Environment.* New York: New York University Press 2004.

"What Miss Hodgkins Says." *New York Sun,* August 6, 1879.

What Was Blackwell's Island? New-York Historical Society Museum & Library. Accessed January 29, 2019; https://www.nyhistory.org/community/blackwells-island.

"Where Is Parson Murray?" *The Sun,* August 2, 1879.

White, Dan. *Under the Stars: How America Fell In Love with Camping.* New York: Henry Holt, 2016.

"The White Wings on Lake Champlain." *Troy Daily Times,* March 23, 1887.

Wilford, John Noble. "How Epidemics Helped Shape the Modern Metropolis." *New York Times,* April 15, 2018.

"Woman Preacher." *The Boston Globe*, March 14, 1895.

Woodlief, Ann. "Ralph Waldo Emerson: 1803–1882." American Transcendentalism Web. Accessed January 29, 2019; http://transcendentalism-legacy.tamu.edu/authors/emerson/.

Yale University. "Yale University Catalogue, 1820." *Yale University Catalogue* 6 (1820). Accessed January 29, 2019; https://elischolar.library.yale.edu/yale_catalogue/6.

———. "Yale University Catalogue, 1827." *Yale University Catalogue* 15 (1827). Accessed January 29, 2019; https://elischolar.library.yale.edu/yale_catalogue/15.

———. "Yale University Catalogue, 1835." *Yale University Catalogue* 21 (1835). Accessed January 29, 2019; https://elischolar.library.yale.edu/yale_catalogue/21.

———. "Yale University Catalogue, 1839." *Yale University Catalogue* 25 (1839). Accessed January 29, 2019; https://elischolar.library.yale.edu/yale_catalogue/25.

———. "*Yale University Catalogue*, 1858." *Yale University Catalogue* 56 (1858). Accessed January 29, 2019; https://elischolar.library.yale.edu/yale_catalogue/56.

———. "*Yale University Catalogue*, 1861." *Yale University Catalogue* 55 (1861). Accessed January 29, 2019; https://elischolar.library.yale.edu/yale_catalogue/55; and "Yale University Catalogue, 1914."

———. "Yale University Catalogue, 1869." *Yale University Catalogue* 59 (1869). Accessed January 29, 2019; https://elischolar.library.yale.edu/yale_catalogue/59.

———. "Yale University Catalogue, 1872." *Yale University Catalogue* 60 (1872). Accessed January 29, 2019; https://elischolar.library.yale.edu/yale_catalogue/60.

Index